3rd Edition

Intermediate

MARKET LEADER

Business English Practice File

John Rogers

American Culture & Language Institute
WD Division, CA 114 Student Services

Contents

Brands

LANGUAGE WORK

VOCABULARY **A** **Use the clues to complete the crossword puzzle.**

Across

2 Something that is .... does not cost a lot to buy or use. (11)

4 An .... brand is one that people think will give them a higher position in society. (12)

7 A .... product has no defects. (4-4)

8 A .... product is attractive and fashionable. (7)

9 If you say that something is a .... product, you think it is very good. (4)

11 .... goods are expensive and intended to appeal to people in a high social class. (8)

Down

1 A..... *classic* ...... product is one that has been popular for a very long time. (7)

3 If a product is .... , it is worth the price you pay for it. (5, 3, 5)

5 If something is .... , you can trust it or depend on it. (8)

6 A .... brand is not affected by changes in fashion. (8)

8 A .... product is fashionable and exciting. (4)

10 If you say that something is .... , you think it is enjoyable. (3)

B **Complete the word partnerships with _brand_, _product_ or _market_.**

1 ..... brand ..... loyalty

2 .... challenger

3 .... endorsement

4 .... stretching

5 .... lifecycle

6 .... share

LANGUAGE REVIEW

A **Complete the sentences with the verbs from the box. Use each verb twice. Put each verb into the correct form and the correct tense – present simple or present continuous.**

invest	sell	take	target	work

1 Breitling and Cartier ......_sell_......... luxury watches around the world.

2 It only .... our laboratory half an hour to test all the ingredients.

3 Which market segment .... they usually .... ?

4 Oh no! My printer .... properly. I'll ask Leila to run off a copy of the report for you.

5 .... you .... more money in marketing this year?

6 Their advertising agency never .... at weekends.

7 Do you think we .... a big risk if we postpone the launch of our new model?

8 Unfortunately, our range of soft drinks .... well at the moment.

9 This time, we .... our advertising campaign on the young.

10 Our company .... a lot in R&D. That's why we develop fewer new products than our competitors.

B **Complete this text with the correct form, present simple or present continuous, of the verbs given. Then check your answers.**

work
manage
develop

work
supervise
write

enjoy
expand / have
own
increase
become

Ralf Hinze _works_ [1] in the R&D department of the Antwerp-based company Merlin Foods Ltd, where he .... [2] a team of five responsible for all organic products under the brand name *Sunnyvale*. They .... [3] about three new products each year.

This week, however, Ralf is not in his office. He .... [4] in the lab. He .... [5] the testing of an innovative range of soups and dressings, and .... [6] a report.

He .... [7] his job and is proud of his company. Indeed, Merlin Foods .... [8] rapidly. It .... [9] subsidiaries in France and Germany and .... [10] Kilkenny Dairies (Ireland). Sales and earnings for the company .... [11] far beyond expectations. The Sunnyvale brand in particular .... [12] hugely popular throughout Europe.

C **Study the information in Exercise B. Then write questions for these answers.**

1 .....*Where does Ralf Hinze work?*.....
In the R&D department at Merlin Foods Ltd.

2 ....
About three each year.

3 ....
In the laboratory.

4 ....
He's supervising the testing of some new products.

5 ....
No, he isn't. He's writing a report.

6 ....
In France and Germany.

7 ....
Yes, indeed. Far beyond expectations!

LANGUAGE + **D** **Tick the ten verbs which are not *normally* found in continuous forms. The first one has been done for you.**

1	agree	☑	8	prefer	☐
2	believe	☐	9	realise	☐
3	belong	☐	10	research	☐
4	compare	☐	11	seem	☐
5	consist	☐	12	stretch	☐
6	contain	☐	13	suppose	☐
7	depend	☐	14	surprise	☐

E **Choose verbs from Exercise D to complete the sentences. Put them into the correct form of the present simple.**

1 It ..... *seems* .... that our new range of equipment is becoming more and more popular.

2 .... he .... to our proposal?

3 Dreher has developed a new brand of beer that .... any alcohol.

4 We may or we may not expand into China. It .... on the success of our products there.

5 Our new range of toiletries .... essentially of environment-friendly deodorant sprays.

6 .... all the respondents .... to the same market segment?

WRITING **A** **Read the passage below about brands and passion.**

In most of the lines **1–13** there is **one extra word** which does not fit.
Some lines, however, are correct.

If a line is **correct**, put a tick (✓) in the space provided.

If there is an **extra word** in the line, write that word in the space.

Companies must try either to make products that a few people love or products	1 ....✓..........
that many people quite like. An attempt to do both will not produce obstacles and	2 ....*not*..........
conflicts. Two things that lie behind the craze for emotional involvement. The first	3 ....
is overcapacity: if there are too many products in every market segment, and this	4 ....
means it is hard to get attention for anything ordinary. Marketing consultants argue	5 ....
that it is not enough for companies to make up their consumer goods just a little	6 ....
better. Instead of, they should make only remarkable things that will make	7 ....
consumers take notice. The second factor is the increased ability of consumers	8 ....
to communicate their views about products, either good or bad. According to some	9 ....
experts, the Internet has increased by a factor of 10 the number of people and that one	10 ....
consumer can influence. Sometimes, companies take an advantage of this by using	11 ....
buzz marketing: they create a group of people who will generate enthusiasm for their	12 ....
products, for example by talking about them in our chat rooms.	13 ....

B **Stan Wouters, Sunnyvale Brand Manager at Merlin Foods Ltd, receives this e-mail from Liz Jansen, Managing Director of the company. Read the message, then write Stan's reply using his notes below.**

LANGUAGE WORK

From:	Liz Jansen
To:	Stan Wouters
Subject:	Sunnyvale range

Hi Stan,

Sales of our range of soups under the Sunnyvale label are increasing month after month in France but are unfortunately falling rapidly in Germany, both in the North and the South.

Jan Kluis, our sales representative in that region, informs me that German customers find our products expensive – when they can find them at all!

I'd be grateful if you could look into the matter and let me have your recommendations as soon as you can.

Many thanks,

Liz

Stan's notes

The largest supermarket chain sells its own
brand of soups at a much lower price
+ don't display our products properly
Our packaging very similar to current market
leader in Germany
Competitors offer frequent discounts
+ visit supermarkets very often

Recommendations:

Jan doing a great job but why alone?
Redesign packaging / highlight brand's qualities
(natural ingredients)
Offer managers incentives for them to
put our products on top shelves
Discounts / special promotions / etc.

VOCABULARY

A **Complete the sentences with words from the box.**

divert	jet-lag	cabin	legroom
delays	~~service~~	flights	

1 A growing number of people criticise the airlines and demand better .... *service* ..... .

2 There are signs that airlines are trying to respond to customer dissatisfaction, for example by providing more .... and quality in-flight meals.

3 Cases of passenger misbehaviour are unfortunately all too common on long-distance ....

4 After a 15-hour flight, you can expect a lot of travellers to suffer from ....

5 Poor service and frequent .... will inevitably harm an airline's reputation.

6 Flight and .... crews sometimes have to deal with dangerous in-flight behaviour.

7 We were heading for Warsaw, but owing to the bad weather, they had to .... our flight to Frankfurt.

B **Complete the text with the best words.**

Customer satisfaction

For the second time, the Korona Hotel has been ranked No. 1 for customer satisfaction.

'At our hotel, we give our .... b ....[1] more than a high-quality experience, we get them to enjoy the Korona way of life,' says Kurt Ahlberg, the General Manager, 'and we pride ourselves on excellent ......[2] in a luxurious environment'.

The ......[3] are responsive and service-oriented, they obviously enjoy their jobs and want to help the clients. The Korona is committed to meeting the ......[4] of today's international business ......[5]: there is high-speed Internet access throughout the hotel, and there are three spacious meeting rooms, with all the ......[6] needed for successful business ......[7].

In addition, the ......[8] of the hotel is ideal: a three-minute drive from the international airport.

Ahlberg has long understood that busy executives cannot afford to waste time in ......[9] jams as they try to ......[10] city centre venues. Nor do executives particularly enjoy getting up at dawn to catch an early-morning ......[11].

1	a) customers	b) guests	c) tourists	d) shoppers
2	a) waiters	b) help	c) chefs	d) service
3	a) crew	b) assistants	c) salesmen	d) staff
4	a) needs	b) functions	c) success	d) failure
5	a) tourists	b) dealers	c) travellers	d) voyagers
6	a) tools	b) facilities	c) buildings	d) machines
7	a) speeches	b) lectures	c) presentations	d) talks
8	a) location	b) place	c) venue	d) situation
9	a) transport	b) street	c) road	d) traffic
10	a) reach	b) get	c) arrive	d) go
11	a) arrival	b) airport	c) flight	d) check-in

C **Use the clues to complete the crossword puzzle.**

Across

1 Line, in British English *(BrE)*. (5)

3 Underground, in American English *(AmE)*. (6)

5 Bill, *AmE*. (5)

6 .... travel is when the largest number of people are travelling. (4)

9 Round trip, *BrE*. (6)

10 Schedule, *BrE*. (9)

Down

2 Lift, *AmE*. (8)

4 A........................ pass is a card that you show before you get on a plane. (8)

5 Parking lot, *BrE*. (3, 4)

7 A........................ is a room in a hotel or airport where people can sit and relax. (6)

8 One way, *BrE*. (6)

LANGUAGE WORK

LANGUAGE REVIEW

A Match each item on the left with an item on the right.

1 As you know, we**'re going to increase** our special offers.

2 We**'re leaving** at five o'clock on Friday morning.

3 Most probably, airport hotels **will become** increasingly popular.

4 Hold on. I**'ll call** our Travel Department and find out for you.

5 Flights **are going to be** delayed again.

a) Look at the fog!

b) They know everything about Apex tickets.

c) They couldn't get us a later flight this time.

d) We're about to start advertising.

e) Many of them have been designed with the business traveller in mind.

B Study the forms in bold in Exercise A. Decide which sentence, 1–5, illustrates each of the meanings, a–e, below.

a) instant decision *sentence 4*

b) pre-planned decision ....

c) prediction based on present evidence ....

d) general prediction / opinion about the future ....

e) future arrangement (diary future) ....

C In each sentence, one word is missing. Show where the word should go and write it on the line provided.

1 Francesca ⟨ travelling from Italy to Singapore in March. *is*

2 We're going meet our agent to discuss our new strategy. ....

3 So you finish in five minutes? OK then. I wait for you in the lounge. ....

4 What time the train arrive in Brussels? ....

5 By the way, Jeff, what you doing on Thursday afternoon? ....

6 It's all decided now. We going to hold the sales conference in Rome. ....

7 Monday morning? Just one moment. I just check my diary. ....

LANGUAGE +

D Put the words and phrases in order to make sentences.

1 as soon as / a ring / I arrive / I'll give / in Brussels. / Mr Dupuis

2 I'll / If / is delayed, / miss / my flight / the presentation.

3 a better hotel. / going to / I find / I'm / stay here / until

4 you advise / I'll / in May / not to go. / our Chinese suppliers / unless / visit / me

5 again. / and visit / you are / in Copenhagen / our headquarters / Please come / when

---

Tip

After *as soon as / if / until / unless / when / once / next time* we use a **present** verb form, even when we are talking about the future.

• Next time you~~'ll be~~ in Vancouver, you must stay at the Plaza Hotel. ✗

• Next time you *are* in Vancouver, you must stay at the Plaza Hotel. ✓

WRITING **A** **Choose the appropriate information from the box to complete the fax from the Atlántida Hotel.**

your arrival	sincerely	look forward to
your departure	faithfully	hope
Dear Mr	However	inform
Dear Ms	As requested	confirm
	We would appreciate it if	request

HOTEL ATLÁNTIDA
Via del Norte, 12
A Coruña, Spain

FAX

From: Hotel Atlántida (A Coruña, Spain)   +34 981 400 123

To: Ms V McDermott, Granta Computer Services Ltd   +44 1865 244 987

April 28

Dear Ms [1] McDermott,

This is to ....[2] your booking for a single room from May 17 to May 20 inclusive, at a rate of 140 euros per night.

................[3], we will hold your room until midnight on the day of ....[4].

We ....[5] seeing you in May.

Yours ....[6],

B **You are going to attend a team-building seminar in Milan.**

Write an e-mail (40–60 words) to your secretary in which you:

- explain why you will be away
- say when exactly you will be away
- give details of what your secretary should do while you are away.

From: **To:** **Subject:**

Change

VOCABULARY **A** **Make prefix and verb combinations to complete the sentences. Use the correct form of the verbs.**

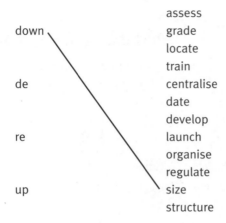

```
down          assess
              grade
              locate
              train
de            centralise
              date
              develop
re            launch
              organise
              regulate
up            size
              structure
```

1   If our company says it's going to ..*downsize*.., I think that means we're out of a job.

2   Could you please .... us on how the project is progressing?

3   Lots of companies say they would like to .... responsibility and authority.

4   Nobody knows what will happen to the company because it has not .... since the last recession.

5   Our company is about to .... its head office to India.

6   Owing to political unrest in the north of the country, many companies began to .... the risk of doing business there.

7   Sales will increase if we .... the product under a different name.

8   In May, the Chinese government announced its plan to .... the telecoms sector into three operators, each with wireless and fixed-line services.

9   The local council has plans to .... the whole area north of our headquarters.

10 We bought the new software and then realised we would need to .... the staff to use it.

11 We want to use the money to .... all our computers with more powerful processors.

12 Our government might .... all internal flights to make the industry more competitive.

VOCABULARY + **B** **All the verbs in Exercise A have a corresponding noun. Make nouns from the verbs and put them in the correct column.**

No change	-ation	-ing	-ment
...*update*...	....	*downsizing*	....
....	....	....	....
....	....	....	....

C **Complete each pair of sentences with the same noun from Exercise B.**

1 The collapse of two banks triggered a widespread .... of the risk of lending money to financial institutions.

   The financial crisis prompted a .... of the banks' role.

2 Mrs Cooper's presidency was marked by the promotion of home ownership, financial .... and an unshakeable faith in the free market.

   Despite the huge problems faced by financial institutions, some experts maintain that further .... of the economy and increased entrepreneurialism are essential for our country to increase its growth rate.

3 Some websites offer a minute-by-minute .... on the rate of exchange between all major currencies.

   The latest .... on fund trends can be downloaded from our website.

4 The retail chain has not yet put a figure on the number of job losses involved in the ....

   Northland Bank could not escape the general .... of staff and branch numbers among the country's major High Street banks.

5 The .... of the product will involve a new brand name and a more attractive label.

   Two months after its .... , the circulation of the newspaper had doubled.

LANGUAGE REVIEW

A **Past simple or present perfect? Use the correct form of the verbs given to complete the conversation.**

René: Alex! What a surprise! I *haven't seen*[1] you for months. *see*

Last time we ....[2] , you ....[3] about to go to Italy. *meet / be*

Alex: That's right, yeah. I ....[4] there to retrain the sales staff at our main subsidiary. *go*

René: Mm. What was that like?

Alex: Interesting, but tough. I'm not sure I ....[5] from the experience yet. *recover*

René: Really? What ....[6] ? *happen*

Alex: Well, one of the guys in the team ....[7] anything that ....[8] like a new idea. *reject* *look*

René: I suppose that's what you call 'resistance to change'.

Alex: Yeah, exactly. And now to make things worse he ....[9] of the team. *drop out*

René: Well, not a big loss, from what you're saying.

Alex: Mm, you're probably right. Anyway. What about you? I've no idea what you ....[10] up to. *be*

René: Guess what! I ....[11] my job! *change*

Alex: What? You ....[12] Klintel? I don't believe you! *quit*

René: Yep! I ....[13] with Orseca since January. *be*

Alex: Oh, I know Orseca. Everyone says it's the place to be.

René: I certainly don't regret my decision. Since I ....[14] working for them, I feel a lot better. And I ....[15] skydiving! *start* *take up*

B **Cross out the incorrect option in each list.**

1   A large number of stores were upgraded
last year.
in the late 1990s.
~~since 2003.~~

2   The concept of the department store was born
in a different era.
over the last few years.
many years ago.

3   It has been an excellent year for Epsol International
so far.
in 2002.
till now.

4   They have
yet
already   reorganised their local business operations.
never

5   How many new products have they launched
since the summer?
this year?
last year?

6   Unfortunately, we didn't redevelop the car park
when we had the money.
for the past three years.
six months ago.

WRITING   **A** **Match each sentence with the correct function on the right.**

1   As agreed, our consultant will be arriving on Wednesday, April 30.

2   Could you please send us some information about the change of ownership at Orseca?

3   If you require any assistance with your relocation, do not hesitate to contact us.

4   This is to let you know that plans for the retraining of our admin staff are under way.

5   We are sorry for any inconvenience you may suffer as a result of this cancellation.

6   We should relaunch our *Davina* mineral water under a different name.

a) apologising
b) confirming
c) informing
d) offering
e) requesting
f) suggesting

B **Match these sentence halves.**

1   According to the latest report our consultant has submitted,

2   Firstly, the timing is far from ideal,

3   In addition, the same employees have sometimes expressed dissatisfaction

4   In my opinion, there are two main

5   Secondly, some employees seem unhappy

6   This is particularly true for seminars

a)   held on Mondays and Fridays.

b)   at the way Jeffrey Hiley conducts the workshops.

c)   attendance at retraining seminars is declining.

d)   especially on Friday after a full working week.

e)   reasons for this situation.

f)   that they were not involved in choosing the topics.

C **Put sentences 1–6 in Exercise B in the correct order to make a section from a report.**

a) ....*1*........ b) .... c) ....

d) .... e) .... f) ....

D **Now complete the next section of the report with items from the box.**

~~recommendations~~	appropriate to	aware of	decisions
in order to	so that		

In order for such seminars to be worth their cost, I would like to make several *recommendations* [1].

Prior to any training programme, we should:

a) carry out an in-depth needs analysis ....[2] ensure that the content of the training is ....[3] the needs of our company;

b) conduct individual interviews with prospective participants, ...[4] we can evaluate their level of motivation;

c) ensure that all staff are fully ....[5] the purpose of the proposed training, and involve them in ....[6] about topics, format and length.

E **Read the passage below about the changing concept of work.**

- In most of the lines **1–10** there is **one extra word** which does not fit. Some lines, however, are correct.
- If a line is **correct**, put a tick (✓) in the space provided.
- If there is an **extra word** in the line, write that word in the space.

For many of us, work is still a place where we go each day. However, the whole   1 ....✓........

concept of a work and leisure is changing, and for an increasing number of people   2 ....*a*........

around the world, work is no longer a place to go but something they do.   3 ....

A substantial number of companies have already introduced a flexible working in policy.   4 ....

This gives their staff a greater degree of choice about when and where they work out.   5 ....

It also enables for them to achieve a balance between their personal and business lives.   6 ....

People with parental responsibilities, for example, value our flexibility enormously.   7 ....

Many companies now offer parents and the option to become 'homeworkers' who finish   8 ....

work early afternoon to spend up the rest of the day with their children, and do the rest of   9 ....

their work when the children are asleep.   10 ....

LANGUAGE WORK

Organisation

VOCABULARY | **A** | **Complete the text with the best words.**

It has become a commonplace to say that the world is changing at an ever-increasing pace. Companies today are faced with a stark choice: .... c .... [1] or go under. For example, four decades ago, companies typically tended to be .... [2]. They were built on a model which achieved a high degree of control, but in which .... [3] of communication were few and slow.

Another disadvantage of this type of organisation is that more junior .... [4] may not even know who the CEO is, or what .... [5] the decision-makers are trying to achieve. In order to try to solve this problem, many organisations have adopted a less .... [6], more flexible business culture in which frequent contact between the owner and the employees ensures that .... [7] is flowing smoothly.

A second difficult choice for a company concerns the extent to which it should go global or remain .... [8]. Global operations allow maximum .... [9] of scale, while localisation makes it possible to .... [10] quickly and to reach all market .... [11]. In order to reduce the tension between global and local demands, many companies have adopted a 'hub and spoke' structure. They use several regional production and .... [12] 'hubs' where neighbouring markets are serviced from one single location.

1	a) adopt	b) market	c) adapt	d) research
2	a) economical	b) hierarchical	c) welcoming	d) democratic
3	a) webs	b) media	c) roads	d) channels
4	a) customers	b) directors	c) staff	d) buyers
5	a) goals	b) design	c) plan	d) sales
6	a) bureaucratic	b) caring	c) decentralised	d) market-driven
7	a) information	b) news	c) speech	d) interest
8	a) professional	b) static	c) local	d) impersonal
9	a) production	b) economies	c) marketing	d) savings
10	a) call	b) demand	c) enquire	d) respond
11	a) shares	b) research	c) leaders	d) sectors
12	a) manufacturing	b) selection	c) distribution	d) advertising

B | **Complete the phrases 1–6 with a verb from the box.**

carry out	~~draw up~~	issue	maintain	train	transport

1 .... *draw up* .... contracts

2 .... goods and equipment

3 install and .... systems

4 .... press releases

5 .... research

6 .... staff

A **Change the following phrases, as in the example.**

1   a hotel with four stars   *a four-star hotel*

2   a deal worth eighty thousand euros   ....

3   a journey that lasts seven hours   ....

4   a loan of two million pounds   ....

5   a seminar that lasts three days   ....

6   an office block that has sixty storeys   ....

B **Match a word from box A with a word from box B to complete the sentences below.**

A	B
computer	commercials
government	fair
information	force
labour	policy
research	project
trade	technology
TV	virus

1   This new *computer virus* could wipe all the data off your hard disk.

2   Several organisations are strongly opposed to the use of children in advertising in general, and in .... in particular.

3   Going to an international .... is often an excellent opportunity for networking.

4   Advances in .... have revolutionised the way people communicate and do business.

5   GVC Steelworks already have a .... of 1,500, and they are still recruiting.

6   The government should commission a special .... to assess the risks posed by GM foods.

7   It would be bad .... to revalue our currency at this particular time.

C **Match the nouns 1–6 with the nouns a–f to make new compounds.**

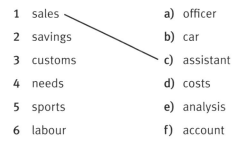

1   sales   a) officer

2   savings   b) car

3   customs   c) assistant

4   needs   d) costs

5   sports   e) analysis

6   labour   f) account

> **Tip**
> In some expressions, the plural –s is kept on the first noun. However, the first noun is usually singular, even when the meaning is plural. For example, *a car manufacturer, a shoe shop.*

D **Use the same word for each group to make new noun combinations.**

1 world ..*trade*..   ..*trade*.. deficit   ..*trade*.. secret

2 crisis m.............   m............. guru   project m.............

3 o............. hours   head o.............   o............. job

4 life i.............   travel i............. policy   i............. broker

5 p............. range   consumer p.............   p............. launch

6 a............. agency   radio a.............   a............. campaign

E **Complete the sentences with words from the box.**

~~level~~	round	breach	waste	lack	range	conflict	cost

1 The ...*level*... of unemployment will soon reach 15%.

2 They accused the striking workers of being in .... of contract.

3 There was a growing .... of interest between her business dealings and her position as a politician.

4 Writing letters by hand is a complete .... of time. I always type them on the computer.

5 Experts forecast that the .... of living will decrease slightly next year.

6 We have pleasure in including further information about our .... of products.

7 We are starting a new .... of negotiations with GVC Steelworks next month.

8 The seminar on 'Motivation at Work' was cancelled through .... of interest.

Tip

Many constructions *noun + of + noun* are relatively fixed. For example:

• *waste of money, lack of interest, show of strength.*

We cannot say ~~money waste~~, ~~interest lack~~ or ~~strength show,~~ for example.

WRITING

A **A large travel agency called *Free Horizons* has recently been reorganised and the new manager, Olivia Anderson, is very keen on staff training. Complete her e-mail with the words from the box.**

~~remain~~	announce	contribute	explain	organise	select

To: All staff
From: O. Anderson
Subject: Staff training

In order to keep our competitive edge, we at *Free Horizons* must continue to provide unique travel services and ...*remain*...[1] totally customer-focused.

Our staff training programmes ....[2] a great deal to making us so dynamic and efficient.

I am very pleased to ....[3] that we will be able to ....[4] another training seminar in the autumn, on one of the following topics:

• developing computer skills,

• intermediate French, Spanish, or Arabic,

• customer service,

• favourite destinations: geography and politics.

Please ....[5] one topic, and ....[6] in detail the reasons for your choice.

Replies by Thursday please.

B **Write a reply (40–55 words) in which you:**

- state your preferred topic
- give reasons for your choice.

To:	O. Anderson
From:	
Subject:	

C **Read the passage below about customer relationship management.**

- In most of the lines **1–10** there is **one extra word** which does not fit. Some lines, however, are correct.
- If a line is **correct**, put a tick (✓) in the space provided.
- If there is an **extra word** in the line, write that word in the space.

Many organisations talk about doing more business electronically, as implementing

cost-cutting measures and improving efficiency. Despite all this talk, some inspired

business leaders have understood what the key of any business connection is: people.

Customers do of course they expect quality products and fair prices, but this is not

the whole story. They also expect to deal with people who have been a positive

attitude, who are enthusiastic about the business if they are in, and who care for them.

Therefore, a growing number of companies have come to realise so that any

transaction can potentially mark the start of a lifelong and relationship. They are now

aware that a large part of the success of any company depends on the quality of

customer services and CRM, which is the short for 'customer relationship management'.

1 .... *as* ....

2 .... ✓ ....

3 ....

4 ....

5 ....

6 ....

7 ....

8 ....

9 ....

10 ....

Advertising

VOCABULARY **A** **Complete each sentence with the best word.**

1 If a celebrity ...*endorses*... a product, they say how good it is in advertisements.

a) persuades   b) launches   c) endorses

2 Billboards, those large signs used for advertising, are often called '........................' in British English.

a) leaflets   b) slogans   c) hoardings

3 Manufacturers of toiletries and cosmetics frequently offer free .... for customers to try out their new products.

a) samples   b) commercials   c) posters

4 Advertising done at the place where a product is sold is called '........................ advertising'.

a) public   b) point-of-sale   c) eye-catching

5 .... of sports or arts events can be a powerful method of advertising.

a) Research   b) Endorsement   c) Sponsorship

6 If you hear about a new product from a friend or relative, this is called '........................ advertising'.

a) word-for-word   b) mouth-to-mouth   c) word-of-mouth

7 Outdoor advertising is growing rapidly due to the rising cost of TV ....

a) commercials   b) publicity   c) research

8 A .... advertisement is one that causes a lot of public discussion and disagreement.

a) viral   b) controversial   c) subliminal

9 'Beanz Meanz Heinz' has become one of the most famous advertising .... ever.

a) slogans   b) banners   c) mailshots

10 The company was forced to withdraw its advertisement because many people found it ....

a) acceptable   b) offensive   c) original

B **Match each verb on the left with two phrases on the right.**

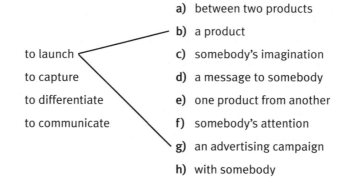

	a) between two products
	b) a product
to launch	c) somebody's imagination
to capture	d) a message to somebody
to differentiate	e) one product from another
to communicate	f) somebody's attention
	g) an advertising campaign
	h) with somebody

A **The passage below is the first part of a text about 'subvertising'.
Complete it with a / an / the. Write Ø if no article is necessary.**

'Subvertising' is ...a... combination of .... words 'subvert' and 'advertising'.
Indeed, subvertising consists of subverting or sabotaging commercial as well as
political advertisements that are displayed in .... public places.

Here is .... simple example: .... advert for .... famous brand
of .... cigarettes depicted .... handsome middle-aged man gazing
thoughtfully into .... distance. .... caption was four words long:
'*The more you know...*'. This ad was easily subverted by someone who just added
.... following words: '*...the less you smoke.*'

B **In the second part of the text, all eight instances of the definite article, *the*,
have been removed. Insert them back where they belong.**

ᵀʰᵉ
ʌ purpose of subvertisers is usually to encourage people to think, not only about
products they buy, but also about nature of society they live in.

There are a number of similarities between advertising and subvertising: both are very
often creative, witty, direct and thought-provoking.

However, differences between two are enormous. While goal of advertising is
ultimately to increase consumption and corporate profits, subvertising aims to make
people aware of constant pressure they are under to buy things, to spend money, to
'shop-till-you-drop', so that they may be able to resist that pressure.

C **In the third and last part of the text, there are no articles. Write in a / an /
the where appropriate.**

ᵃ
In addition, subvertising is ʌ reaction against invasion of public places by hoardings,
posters, slogans, logos, etc., which some say 'pollute our mental environment'.
It is attempt to 'reclaim streets', to free our personal space of those consumerist
messages which can be seen or heard left, right and centre in our cities.

While one cannot ignore that in eyes of law, altering hoardings is considered minor
form of vandalism, one has to recognise that subvertising is form of creativity and way
of exercising one's freedom of speech.

WRITING **A** **Choose the correct item from each pair to complete the letter.**

schedule	~~I have pleasure in~~	We would be very grateful
date and time	I am pleased to	We are delighted
further information	take advantage of	we enclose
full details	look forward to	we could arrange for

SPICA OFFICE SOLUTIONS
12 CONNAUGHT AVENUE, GLASGOW

21 May

Ms Glenda Munroe
Purchasing Manager
United Freight Agencies
Liverpool

Dear Ms Munroe,

As Head of our Customer Service Department, *I have pleasure in.*[1] enclosing our latest catalogue, featuring our exciting new range of office equipment and furniture at the most competitive prices currently on the market.

.............[2] if you could let us know which of our products would be of particular interest to you. Once we have this information, ...[3] an expert from our sales staff to visit your company in order to carry out a detailed needs analysis and produce a unique office solution for you, entirely free of charge.

Our expert would also give you ....[4] of our special offers. At Spica Office Solutions we offer our regular customers more than just discounts. For example, there is a two-month free trial period for all electrical equipment, including photocopiers, and much more.

If you would like to ....[5] a visit from our expert, please inform us of a suitable ....[6].

We look forward to hearing from you.

Yours sincerely,

Ben Costello

Ben Costello
Sales Manager

B **Write a reply to Mr Costello in which you:**

- thank him for the catalogue
- describe what kind of office equipment / furniture you are interested in
- accept his offer of a visit from an expert
- suggest a time and date for the visit.

C **Look at the examples, then match the sentence halves below.**

On average, 2,000 people visit our website every month.

By and large, I think it was a successful advertising campaign.

1 **Basically,** the two products are the same

2 **As a rule,** our advertisements never

3 **Overall,** we are satisfied with the design,

4 **All things considered,** it has been

5 **In general,** we advertise more on the Internet

6 **Roughly speaking,** our website

a) a successful year for Marketing.

b) but we find the colours are rather dull.

c) gets about 800 hits a week.

d) show people drinking alcohol or smoking.

e) though the packaging is completely different.

f) than on radio and TV.

Tip

We often use introductory phrases like the ones in bold when we want to *generalise*. In the second example above, the advertising campaign was successful *generally speaking*, but it was probably not successful *in every single detail*.

D **Read the passage below about junk mail.**

- In each line **1–8** there is **one wrong word**.
- For each line, **underline the wrong word** in the text and **write the correct word** in the space provided.

'Junk mail' is the name given to all the sales ads, catalogues, prize offers, etc. which

find their way into your letterbox without you having requested anything.

While some of that mail gets into everyone's mailbox, the sizeable proportion of it is   1 ....*a*..........

actually personalised and addressed to certain individuals in particularly.   2 ....

Computerised mailing list have made it very easy for companies to obtain huge   3 ....

numbers of names and addresses. When your subscribe to a magazine or buy   4 ....

something from a mail order catalogue, by example, your name is entered into a   5 ....

computers, and very often automatically added to one or more mailing lists. The mail   6 ....

order firm or the credit card company in question can then rent their lists on other   7 ....

companies, and that is when your letterbox began to overflow with unwanted mail.   8 ....

A number of organisations have now been created specifically to help the public deal

with unsolicited advertisements.

Money

VOCABULARY **A** **Use the clues to complete the crossword puzzle.**

Across

1 A company's ….*turnover*…. is the amount of business it does over a certain period of time. (8)

3 A company's sales …………………. is the money it receives from selling goods or services. (7)

5 Money which people or organisations put into a business in order to make a profit. (10)

8 A difficult time for the economy of a country, when there is less business activity. (9)

11 A …………………. is a description of what is likely to happen in the future. (8)

Down

2 An …………………. stake is the money risked when a business owns part of another company. (6)

4 The …………………. is the part of the profits of a company that is paid to shareholders for each share that they own. (8)

6 A …………………. market is where a company's shares are bought and sold. (5)

7 The …………………. margin is the difference between the price of a product or service and the cost of producing it. (6)

9 One of the parts into which ownership of a company is divided. (5)

10 Money that one person, organisation or country owes to another. (4)

B **Cross out the verb which does not normally go with the noun in the bubble.**

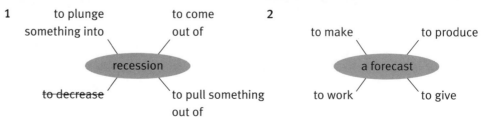

1   to plunge   to come
    something into   out of

recession

~~to decrease~~   to pull something
     out of

2   to make   to produce

a forecast

to work   to give

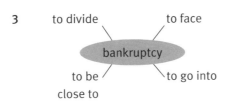

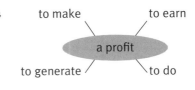

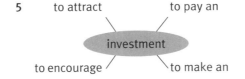

C **Match these sentence halves.**

1 Sales went up beyond expectations, and Kernel Computers made a
2 Our economic experts have produced a
3 Competition is so fierce that many small travel operators are
4 The government has promised to eliminate bureaucracy in order to
5 They spend more than they earn and run up
6 We fear that a rise in interest rates will

a) gloomy sales forecast for the next quarter.
b) encourage foreign investment.
c) plunge the country into recession.
d) record profit of 150 million euros.
e) close to bankruptcy.
f) huge debts on their credit cards.

LANGUAGE REVIEW

A **Complete these pairs of opposites.**

1 to go up   to go d o w n

2 to r _ se   to _ _ _ l

3 to _ _ cr _ _ se to de _ _ _ _ _ _

4 to s _ _ r   to _ _ _ mm _ _

5 to _ _ _ ble   to h _ _ _ e

B **Study these examples and the rule before doing Exercise C.**

● Profitability has risen. ✓

● ~~They have risen sales.~~ ✗

● The banks have raised interest rates by 0.5%. ✓

● ~~Interest rates have raised again.~~ ✗

What's the rule?

We can use some verbs without an object; we call them **intransitive verbs** (I).
We can use other verbs with an object; we call them **transitive verbs** (T).
Profitability has risen: subject + verb with no object
Rise is always an **intransitive** verb.
The banks have raised interest rates by 0.5%: subject + verb + object
Raise is always a **transitive** verb.
Many verbs can be both **transitive** and **intransitive**. For example:
The volume of sales will decrease. (I)
They will decrease the volume of sales. (T)

LANGUAGE WORK

C Mark each verb (I) if you can use it to complete sentence a, (T) if you can use it to complete sentence b, or (I) / (T) if you can use it to complete both.

a) The volume of sales will ....

b) They will .... the volume of sales.

1 fall ......(I)......

2 double ......(I) / (T)......

3 drop ....

4 decline ....

5 halve ....

6 increase ....

7 level off ....

8 peak ....

9 plummet ....

10 soar ....

D Complete the words to make the corresponding adverb for each adjective.

Adjective	Adverb
1 considerable	considera b l y
2 dramatic	dramatic _ _ _ _
3 gradual	gradual _ _
4 sharp	sharp _ _
5 significant	significant _ _
6 slight	sli _ _ _ _ _
7 steady	stea _ _ _ _
8 substantial	substan _ _ _ _ _ _

E The two sentences below have the same meaning. Study the example, then rewrite sentences 1–7 in the same way.

*There was a **considerable increase** in oil prices*   Adjective + noun

means the same as

*Oil prices **increased considerably**.*   Verb + adverb

1 There has been a **dramatic fall** in exports.

2 It seems that there is going to be a **substantial rise** in taxes.

3 There was a **steady rise** in the number of people out of work.

4 Are you saying that there is a **significant decline** in production?

5 I think domestic demand will **fall slightly**.

6 Profit **grew gradually**.

7 Orders have **dropped sharply**.

WRITING

A Match items 1–5 with items a–e.

1 **Despite** the rising euro and falling sales,

2 The euro rose and sales fell slightly,

3 Vegaco's profits did not remain constant

4 Their competitors' profits increased

5 The strong euro affected all software companies.

a) **although** they were affected by the strong euro as well.

b) **because** of the strong euro and a slight fall in sales.

c) **However**, the profits of Vegaco's competitors did not decrease.

d) **so** Vegaco's profits did not reach the same level as in the previous quarter.

e) Vegaco's profits did not fall significantly.

B **Study the linking words in bold in Exercise A. Then use each linking word twice to complete the following sentences.**

1 Sales of our range of fruit juices improved ..... *because* ..... we made the packaging more attractive.

2 As you can see from the graph, sales did very well in the second quarter. Since June, ..., there has been a gradual drop.

3 Profits continued to rise .... a slight increase in production costs.

4 We plan to centralise distribution, ... costs are likely to decrease.

5 September can be a difficult month .... sales often fall after the summer holiday.

6 .... the booming market for mobile communications, Alfitel's share price fell steadily.

7 We have just relaunched the XL30 under a different name, ... sales will probably go up.

8 .... our production costs have gone down by 3%, profits have not improved significantly.

9 We launched our advertising campaign three months ago. ...., sales have not recovered yet.

10 Profits went up .... sales did not seem to improve.

C **Read the passage below about the unequal distribution of wealth.**

- In most of the lines **1–11** there is **one extra word** which does not fit. Some lines, however, are correct.
- If a line is **correct**, put a tick (✓) in the space provided.
- If there is an **extra word** in the line, write that word in the space.

Most news programmes now have a business section. This might give us the

illusion that we are all equally affected by stock markets and financial speculation.

When we care to study the facts and figures, however, it will soon becomes clear   1 .... *will* ....

that the glamorous financial deals we regularly hear about benefit to only a tiny   2 ....

minority of people. According to a recent report published in the US, the   3 ....

wealthiest 1% of the population control more than one third of all the nation's wealth.   4 ....

This concentration of wealth among the very rich and has mostly remained   5 ....

constant over the past ten years. On the other one hand, the living standards of a   6 ....

large proportion of the population have stagnated or declined. This kind   7 ....

phenomenon is by no means unique to the US, it is indeed a common throughout   8 ....

the industrialised world well. It is also occurring in emerging economies like India   9 ....

and China. As the gap between average families and not the very few ultra-rich   10 ....

continues to widen, it seems urgent to address the issue of global inequality of   11 ....

wealth and income distribution.

Cultures

VOCABULARY

A Complete the idioms in the sentences below with the correct word.

1 We don't agree what or when we should advertise. In fact, it seems we don't see .... to eye on anything at all.

2 In many countries, people make a comment about the weather to .... the ice and start a conversation.

3 I'd just told my hosts I hated fish when it turned out they'd spent hours making fish soup, one of their national dishes. I had really put my .... in it.

4 I didn't know exactly how long I had for my presentation, and I knew nothing about the audience. The organisers had really thrown me in at the .... end.

5 After a few minutes we found we had loads of things in common. We just got .... like a house on fire.

B Put the words in the correct order to make idioms.

1 to / water / into / hot / get

2 to / opener / real / a / be / eye-

3 to / out / fish / feel / water / a / of / like

C Use an idiom from Exercise B in the correct form to complete these sentences.

1 That business trip to China .... for me. That's when I began to understand the culture.

2 Don't be late for the departmental meeting, or you

.... with the boss.

3 I really .... at the reception. Very few people spoke English, and those who did, didn't have much to say.

VOCABULARY +

D Complete the sentences with a preposition from the box.

~~out~~	over	up	in	with	of

1 Leo's been to Nigeria many times. He knows the culture inside ...*out*....

2 We've told you everything about this job opportunity in Uzbekistan. Now *you* tell us what you think. The ball is .... your court.

3 Sometimes it doesn't really matter if you don't know the culture. You just need to maintain a good-natured attitude and go .... the flow.

4 Because she has a very good grasp .... Russian, Linda quickly became integrated into the local community when she moved to Omsk.

5 If any of the presentations runs .... schedule, we'll be late for the final plenary meeting.

6 With this conference next month, we're all .... to our eyes in work at the office.

E **Match the idioms from Exercise D with the correct explanation.**

1 the ball is in your court

2 to be up to one's eyes in work

3 to go with the flow

4 to have a good / poor grasp of something

5 to know something inside out

6 to run over schedule

a) to be relaxed and not worry about what you should do

b) it is your responsibility to take action next

c) to be very familiar with something

d) to have a lot / too much to do

e) to take more time than expected

f) to be able / unable to understand something well

LANGUAGE REVIEW

A **Match these sentence halves.**

1 All foreign nationals *must*

2 Although it is quite a liberal country,

3 In their meetings, junior staff *have to*

4 They have 'casual Fridays', which means

5 You *mustn't* take more than

6 You *shouldn't* buy a very expensive gift,

a) let senior executives speak first.

b) fill in a landing card.

c) the equivalent of 1,000 euros out of the country.

d) otherwise you could embarrass your hosts.

e) you *don't have to* wear formal clothes on that day.

f) you *should* avoid drinking alcohol in public.

B **Study the example sentences in Exercise A, and answer these questions.**

1 Which two sentences express advice? [2] and [ ]

2 Which sentence expresses the idea that it is not necessary to do something? [ ]

3 Which sentence expresses the idea that something is against the law? [ ]

4 Which sentence expresses the idea that something is required by law? [ ]

5 Which sentence expresses the idea that something is required by social 'rules'? [ ]

C **Complete these sentences with *have to* / *don't have to* / *mustn't*.**

1 In Britain, you ...*have to*... pay tax on the interest that your money earns.

2 In most countries, you still .... pay to use public transport.

3 You .... drink alcohol during working hours.

4 In some countries, motorists are lucky: they .... pay a toll to use motorways.

5 You .... take home any office stationery or equipment. If you do, you may lose your job.

6 In most European countries, you .... have an identity card on you at all times.

7 In the United States, you .... make a lot of small talk. Americans usually like to get down to business quickly.

8 In many countries, you .... ask about a businesswoman's marital status. It is considered rude.

D **Rewrite these sentences using an appropriate modal form to replace the words in *italics*.**

1 *It is not necessary for you to* wear a suit. Their company culture is quite informal.

...... You don't have to wear a suit. ......

2 *You are not allowed to* drive without your seat belt on.

....

3 If you are invited for dinner, *it is a good idea if you* buy your hosts some flowers.

....

4 In many countries, *it is not good to* point your finger at people.

....

5 Although I know them all very well, I *am obliged to* address my colleagues by their surname.

....

6 *It is essential* for all visitors to wear their name badge at all times.

....

7 *Is it necessary* for me to buy my hosts an expensive gift?

....

8 In Canada, smoking *is prohibited* in most public spaces.

....

WRITING **A** **Sentences 1–10 below are from two different documents. Decide which are from a) a letter of invitation to a consultant, and b) an e-mail booking. Write the sentence numbers in the table in the correct order.**

a)	Letter of invitation to training consultant	5				
b)	Informal e-mail requesting booking	6				

1 As I explained to you briefly when we met, our engineers often spend periods of up to three months in India, Malaysia or the Philippines.

2 Breakfast only please as they'll be otherwise entertained for the rest of the day.

3 Could you book three single rooms en suite in my name at the Royal, 3–6 May?

4 I very much hope that your schedule will allow you to accept our invitation.

5 I was delighted to talk to you after your presentation at the *Bridging the Culture Gap* conference in Frankfurt last week, and I would like to thank you for the interest you expressed in our company.

6 Just to let you know that we are expecting three potential clients from Egypt to visit our design department early next month.

7 Many of them request practical information about various aspects of those cultures.

8 Many thanks.

9 That reminds me: any suggestions for their evening programme would be greatly appreciated.

10 We would therefore like to invite you to run a one-day training seminar on cultural issues for a group of twelve staff due to leave for the Philippines in mid-April.

B **Complete the reply to the letter in Exercise A with items from the box.**

Further to your letter	I look forward to
as you suggested	owing to previous engagements
As you probably know	convenient for you
if you could let me know	I would be delighted

LANGUAGE WORK

Further to your letter [1] of January 10, I would like to thank you for your kind invitation.

.... [2] to run a one-day seminar for your staff.

.... [3], I have first-hand experience of the Asia–Pacific region, and it is always a great pleasure for me to run seminars focusing specifically on that area.

However, ... [4], I am afraid that I could not possibly run a workshop in March .... [5].

I would be grateful .... [6] whether late February or early April would be .... [7].

.... [8] hearing from you in due course.

C **Read the passage below about cross-cultural awareness.**

- In most of the lines **1–11** there is **one extra word** which does not fit. Some lines, however, are correct.
- If a line is **correct**, put a tick (✓) in the space provided.
- If there is an **extra word** in the line, write that word in the space.

It is sometimes said that cultures are becoming more alike under the effect of

mass tourism and globalisation.

However, there often remains a gap between any two given cultures.   1 ....✓..........

What enables for us to bridge this gap is often called *cultural awareness*. Empathy,   2 ....*for*.......

i.e. openness of mind and heart together with a willingness to try and understand   3 ....

things from someone else's perspective, is a necessary condition and for such an   4 ....

awareness to develop. However, empathy on its own it is not enough. We also   5 ....

need that to develop an ability to look at our culture from the outside. This process   6 ....

should make us realise that all the behaviours, beliefs and values that we have   7 ....

always taken in for granted may indeed appear strange to someone from another   8 ....

cultural group. In our other words, we need to be able both to make the strange look   9 ....

familiar, and they make the familiar look strange. If we can achieve this, then we can   10 ....

develop about what some sociologists call our cultural awareness.   11 ....

Human resources

VOCABULARY **A** Complete the sentences with items from the box.

resume	applicant	a covering letter	shortlist	a vacancy
a headhunter	permanent	interview	a probationary period	a reference

1 The usual American English word for 'CV' is '...*resume*...'.

2 Exlon has hired .... to attract talented executives from rival companies.

3 We ask all our new employees to work .... of between one and three months.

4 The starting salary of the successful .... will be decided on the basis of qualifications and experience.

5 The panel will .... candidates for interview and contact them by the end of the week.

6 Please send .... together with your CV.

7 Our company has .... for a graduate in economics.

8 When you apply for a job, you can ask your previous employer for ....

9 A survey showed that most temporary workers were hoping to be offered a .... post.

10 Applicants will be called for .... between 15 and 25 May.

VOCABULARY + **B** Cross out the verb which does not normally go with the noun in the bubble.

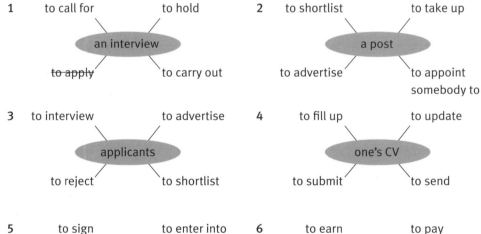

1
to call for   to hold
an interview
to apply   to carry out

2
to shortlist   to take up
a post
to advertise   to appoint somebody to

3
to interview   to advertise
applicants
to reject   to shortlist

4
to fill up   to update
one's CV
to submit   to send

5
to sign   to enter into
a contract
to terminate   to work

6
to earn   to pay
a salary
to receive   to submit

LANGUAGE REVIEW

A **Match these sentence halves.**

1 If the candidate is highly qualified, of course we don't mind

2 If your probationary period is successful, we promise

3 The job is so dull that I'm considering

4 They want candidates with lots of experience because they can't afford

5 Tony was upset because his previous employer refused

6 We can't fill the vacancy this month because we have put off

a) to train new staff.

b) to give him a reference.

c) to offer you a permanent post.

d) paying a more competitive salary.

e) advertising it for far too long.

f) handing in my resignation.

B **Complete the sentences with either the infinitive or -ing form of the verb to advertise.**

1 We plan *to advertise* all our vacancies on our website.

2 This vacancy needs to be filled urgently, so don't delay ....

3 There aren't a lot of enquiries because we forgot .... in the local paper.

4 The board have decided .... the post of Deputy HR Manager more widely.

5 I think we should stop .... in The Westland Echo. They're far too expensive.

C **Correct the two sentences which are grammatically wrong.**

1 When I suggested to hire more part-time staff, nobody listened to me.

2 Unfortunately, my previous employer failed to provide the reference I needed.

3 If you want your covering letter to be accurate, I recommend doing at least one spell check.

4 I must remember calling the job centre to enquire about part-time jobs.

5 I have arranged to see the HR manager tomorrow morning.

LANGUAGE +

D **Put the items in the correct order to make sentences.**

1 to take / action / were threatening / industrial / the unions

2 to raise / they / by two per cent / offered / my salary

3 to be / I / next year / my line manager / promoted / expect / I've told

4 to favour / younger candidates / I thought / tended / the interviewer

5 to relocate / that / I'm / my company / worried / intends

6 to represent / claims / of our workforce / the union / over sixty per cent

E **Complete the sentences with the correct preposition.**

1 We look forward .... hearing from you.

2 Please read the contract carefully .... signing it.

3 We are thinking .... hiring some part-time workers.

4 The unions are firmly opposed .... any redundancies.

5 They were all in favour .... relocating production to Romania.

LANGUAGE WORK

WRITING **A** **Complete the job advertisement with items from the box.**

recruiting for	fluent	short-listed candidates	CV
an interview	remuneration	successful applicant	
applications	responsible to	well-qualified	

– AGRIBANK –

Chief IT Officer (CITO)

Agribank, one of the three leading banks in the country, is
..*recruiting for* ..[1] an exceptionally ....[2] IT specialist to
manage the development of software, deployment of hardware, and support
of various computing technologies at its headquarters and its eight regional
branches.

Duties and responsibilities:

The CITO is ....[3] the General Manager for the satisfactory
performance of all technology functions performed within the country:

- Management of Agribank IT staff
- Software development activities
- Software and hardware maintenance activities
- Long-range technology planning

The ....[4] will be ....[5] in English and German.
We offer an attractive ....[6] package and long-term career
prospects.
Interested candidates should send their letter of application and
....................[7] via e-mail to Erna Asselborn at hrm@agribank.com
Closing date for ....[8]: Friday, 3 June.
Only ....[9] will be contacted for ....[10].

B Nancy Oberweis is applying for the post described in Exercise A. Put the sentences (a–h) in the correct order to write her e-mail to Agribank.

From: Nancy.Oberweis@pt.lu
To: hrm@agribank.com

a) Dear Ms Asselborn, ☐ 1

b) The aim of the project is to equip the Ministry of Finance with up-to-date computer systems, develop adequate software, and support the local IT staff responsible for technology planning. ☐

c) Finally, please do not hesitate to contact me if you need any further details. ☐

d) With the benefit of all the experience I have gained there, I now look forward to a challenge and a steady career in my home country. If I am short-listed, could you please let me know whether you would be willing to consider a telephone interview. ☐

e) I look forward to hearing from you.

f) I am enjoying all these responsibilities tremendously. However, the project will be completed in three months' time and I will therefore leave Bulgaria. ☐

g) Since September 2007, I have been working as IT consultant on a UN-sponsored project in Bulgaria. ☐

h) With reference to your advertisement in the Luxembourg Daily News of May 10, I would like to apply for the post of Chief IT Officer. As you can see from the attached CV, I obtained my MSc in mathematics and computer science from Imperial College London in July 2007. ☐

Yours sincerely,
Nancy Oberweis

C Read the passage below about the human consequences of redundancies.

- In each line **1–9** there is **one wrong word**.
- For each line, **underline the wrong word** in the text, and **write the correct word** in the space provided.

Articles about redundancies frequently focus on numbers and statistics and tend to ignore the psychological impact of job losses.

Naturally, reactions on redundancies vary from one individual to another and | 1 ....to.........
depend for age and the number of years spent with the company, among other | 2 ....
factors. However, most of the victims initially feel disbelief, than anger and | 3 ....
depression. Indeed, such a change in there professional circumstances can have | 4 ....
a devastatingly effect on their home lives and family relationships. Very often, | 5 ....
for example, losing one's job means having to relocate, sometime far away | 6 ....
from one's relatives and closed friends. In addition, redundancies also have | 7 ....
long-lasting effect on those who survive them. Survivors often feel guilty | 8 ....
about being luckiest than those who had to go, betrayed by management, and | 9 ....
frightened of being next in line.

VOCABULARY **A** **Use the clues to complete the crossword puzzle.**

Across

2 The practice of selling products at a very low price in an export market. (7)

4 They separate countries and can make trade more difficult. (7)

7 Limited numbers or amounts that are officially allowed. (6)

8 Taxes paid on goods coming into or going out of a country. (7)

9 A general word which covers all things which stop people trading freely. (8)

Down

1 To give money to a company or industry to make a product cheaper to buy or produce. (9)

2 The removal or reduction of government controls on a particular business activity. (12)

3 A situation in which goods come into and out of a country without any controls or taxes. (4, 5)

5 Government department responsible for collecting taxes on goods. (7)

6 To bring something into a country from abroad, usually in order to sell it. (6)

VOCABULARY + **B** **Complete each set of sentences with the same item.**

1 We are glad to inform you that your .... *order* .... is being processed.

Considering that delivery is already two weeks overdue, I am afraid we have to cancel our .... *order* .....

This is the first time we have placed an .... *order* .... with Benson & Kay.

2 Without a wage index system, workers are not .... against inflation.

Global banking has changed from being a .... industry to a deregulated one.

In the past, the Mexican government .... its domestic growers by regulating corn imports.

3 They have .... us a very good price for the consignment.

The hotel .... us a special rate because our staff use it on a regular basis.

A number of football clubs are now .... on the Stock Exchange.

4 It is essential that you comply with government ....

Our company is going to introduce tighter health and safety ....

Our government has once again breached the .... governing the sale of weapons.

5 Our usual supplier was unable to .... the delivery date.

We are sorry to inform you that the programme you propose does not .... our requirements

Two of our colleagues have failed to .... their performance target.

6 Kentoril is trying to break into the Chinese ....

We plan to put our new model on the .... next winter.

They fear that Central Asian countries will flood the .... with cheap goods.

7 It is useful to .... a market survey before you make a major investment.

We are very satisfied with our new supplier. They always .... our instructions in every detail.

We always .... rigorous tests on our new products.

LANGUAGE REVIEW

A Match these sentence halves.

1 I think that if you offer them some concessions,

2 If I didn't win so many deals,

3 If they bothered to pay promptly,

4 If they pay within 30 days,

5 If we give you a larger discount,

6 If we were able to give you a larger discount,

7 If you paid late,

8 If your payment is overdue,

9 Perhaps if you offered them some concessions,

10 Unless I win this deal,

a) would you make a firm order?

b) will you make a firm order?

c) they'll do the same.

d) they'd do the same.

e) we'd offer a 5% cash discount.

f) we'll offer a 5% cash discount.

g) we'll have to close your account.

h) we'd have to close your account.

i) my commission will decrease.

j) my commission would decrease.

B Complete the sentences with 'll, 'd, won't or wouldn't.

1 We ...d... give you a more substantial discount if you paid cash.

2 If they didn't find our terms satisfactory, they .... continue doing business with us.

3 So if we order 200 units, you .... give us a 10% discount, is that right?

4 We .... be able to order more if you can't deliver within a week.

5 If you can't deliver this week, we .... have to turn to another supplier.

6 We .... have to look for another supplier if you were able to dispatch immediately.

7 I'm sure we .... get this contract unless we offer a lower price.

8 If I were you, I .... look for a more reliable supplier.

LANGUAGE WORK

C **Choose the correct alternative to complete these sentences.**

1 We might be able to increase the size of our order | if / ~~unless~~ | you agreed to a higher discount.

2 As long as / In case / Unless | you can guarantee prices for the next two years, we'll sign the contract.

3 Provided that / Unless | you agree to cover insurance as well, we've got a deal.

4 We'll never be able to solve this problem | if / unless / as long as | we agree to discuss it right now.

5 We're looking for an alternative supplier | in case / providing | our usual one can't deliver next week.

6 I'm afraid we won't be able to place a firm order | unless / provided / if | you agree to split the transport costs.

WRITING **A** **Complete the letter with items from the box.**

a) ~~a range of mountaineering equipment~~

b) receiving your acknowledgement

c) and delivered within the next six weeks

d) and your invoice direct to us

e) by letter of credit at 30 days

f) in the hope of more favourable terms in future

g) please do not send substitutes instead

L'ILLIMANI

27 rue des Charmes, 1000 Brussels   Tel: +32 (2) 541 1609   Fax: +32 (2) 541 1608

Mr P Canetti
Italmont S.p.A
Via Degli Ausoni 23
11100 Aosta
Italy

26 May

Dear Mr Canetti,

Please find enclosed our order No. TW526 for ...a...[1].

Although we find your trade discount of 10% rather low, we are placing a fairly large order this time ....[2].

As agreed, we would like the goods to be sent by rail freight ....[3].

Payment will be ....[4]. Would you please send the shipping documents ....[5].

If any of the listed items are not available, ...[6].

We look forward to ....[7].

Yours sincerely,

Eric Lambert

Eric Lambert
Store Manager

B Study this reply to the letter in Exercise A. One error has been marked; find five more.

Italmont S.p.A

Via Degli Ausoni 23
11100 Aosta
Italy

Mr E Lambert
L'Illimani
27   (72) rue des Charmes
1000 Brussels

30 April

Mr Lambert,

Thank you for your order No. TW526 which we received today.

It is now being processed and should be ready for dispatch within the next three months. I am pleased to be able to confirm already that we have all the items in stock.

In due course, the shipping documents and our invoice will be sent to your bank as you requested.

Yours faithfully,

Paolo Canetti

C Read the passage below about global trade.

- In most of the lines **1–10** there is **one extra word** which does not fit. Some lines, however, are correct.
- If a line is **correct**, put a tick (✓) in the space provided.
- If there is an **extra word** in the line, write that word in the space.

About two decades ago, the supporters of globalisation have promised that free trade	1 ..... *have* ....
would bring a prosperity to people in both developed and developing countries.	2 ....
As more and more governments enter the WTO–IMF sphere of influence, however,	3 ....
the economic difficulties they face and lead to the conclusion that those promises	4 ....
were grossly exaggerated. An increasing number of companies outsource or relocate to	5 ....
countries where labour is cheaper, environmental laws more weaker and workers' rights	6 ....
fewer. As a result, millions of people have, especially in developing countries, work	7 ....
in sweatshop conditions, labouring for all day in unsafe and unhealthy conditions	8 ....
for meagre wages. On the other hand, a very huge number of manufacturing workers in	9 ....
developed countries have lost decently-paid jobs as companies have moved to overseas	10 ....
in search of lower production costs.	

VOCABULARY **A** **Complete the sentences with words from the box.**

corruption	discrimination	fixing	fraud	espionage
testing	trading	laundering	counterfeit	pollution

1 European companies have developed a code of ethics to improve the defence industry's reputation, after allegations of bribery and …*corruption*… in connection with some of its biggest names.

2 A California-based computer medical simulation company has developed a system to predict the effects of cosmetics on human skin, cutting the need for animal ………………… .

3 The EU investigated international telephone agreements to see if there was price ………………… in violation of EU competition rules.

4 The national commission on environmental ………………… recommended that a third of the country's fishing waters be designated conservation zones, where fishing would be banned until stocks recovered.

5 The government says sex ………………… is damaging to the economy and plans to bolster workers' rights.

6 Our rival's summer collection has items so similar to our own new design that we think this might be a case of industrial ………………… .

7 The global watchdog on criminal fund flows is investigating claims that football clubs and other sports teams are being used as a conduit for money ………………… .

8 China is the biggest source of ………………… goods in the world.

9 Mr Dubuisson was fined €30,000 for 'a minor tax ………………… ' in Finland after failing to declare €11,000 worth of imported goods on arrival in Helsinki from Switzerland.

10 Because shares in both banks jumped 20% two weeks before confirmation of their merger, an insider ………………… enquiry was opened.

VOCABULARY + **B** **Complete each sentence with the best word.**

1 Some of our sales representatives were …*accused*… of offering bribes.

   a) arrested   **b)** accused   **c)** charged

2 She was ………………… to three years in prison for the laundering of drug profits.

   a) sentenced   **b)** arrested   **c)** investigated

3 A former Goldman Brothers executive has recently been ………………… with insider trading.

   a) convicted   **b)** charged   **c)** wanted

4 If the builders don't fulfil their side of the contract, we'll ………………… .

   a) sentence   **b)** acquit   **c)** sue

5 Few people ………………… Fleur de Lys Cosmetics of animal testing.

   a) suspected   **b)** prosecuted   **c)** committed

6 The airline had .... potential investors about its financial difficulties.

    a) misinformed   **b)** undermined   **c)** lied

7 The director was found guilty of .... the true position of his accounts.

    a) lying   **b)** cheating   **c)** misrepresenting

8 The company .... the government by €25,000 for labour and materials.

    a) stole   **b)** overcharged   **c)** mistreated

9 Some airlines offer cash as compensation for passengers when flights are ....

    a) misused   **b)** discredited   **c)** overbooked

10 It is illegal for employers to .... on grounds of race, sex or religion.

    a) discriminate   **b)** distinguish   **c)** discredit

LANGUAGE REVIEW

A **Past simple, past continuous or past perfect? Complete the text with the correct form of the verbs in brackets.**

Sharon Embley ...*started*...[1] (*start*) working as Deputy Marketing Manager for Fleur de Lys Cosmetics three years ago. It was the kind of job she ....[2] (*always / want*). Competition for the post ....[3] (*be*) really tough, and she knew she ....[4] (*be*) selected because of her experience in marketing, which she ....[5] (*gain*) in her previous job with a pharmaceuticals company.

Sharon ....[6] (*be*) young and ambitious. She was also a person of absolute moral integrity. In fact, she ....[7] (*apply*) for this post with Fleur de Lys mainly because the company ....[8] (*pride*) itself on its ethical business practices. Its image was built on natural ingredients, environment-friendly packaging, and a ban on animal testing. This image ....[9] (*reflect*) the values which Sharon ....[10] (*always / cherish*).

Things ....[11] (*go*) really well, until one day a file ....[12] (*land*) on her desk. She ....[13] (*not / know*) the file was not meant for her, or that it ....[14] (*contain*) confidential information. She ....[15] (*read*) it all, and ....[16] (*discover*) to her amazement that Fleur de Lys was not as 'clean' as it claimed to be. It ....[17] (*be*) true that they did not test their products on animals, but only because they did not need to: other laboratories ....[18] (*already / test*) the ingredients on animals!

Ironically, the day before she ....[19] (*read*) the report, the director ....[20] (*call*) her to her office. She ....[21] (*inform*) Sharon that she ....[22] (*plan*) to promote her very soon as the current Marketing Manager was due to retire.

Sharon ....[23] (*not / experience*) such confusion for a long time. What should she do? If she ....[24] (*blow*) the whistle, she would not get promoted and might even be dismissed. And if she ....[25] (*keep*) silent ...

B **Match these conversation excerpts.**

1 Has Joe ever done anything illegal?

2 Have you heard of Alex recently?

3 Why has he given the contract to the most expensive supplier?

4 He's always been respected for his principles.

5 I've never made a single personal call from the office, you know.

6 So you've worked for Wilson Engineering since 1991.

a) That's right. Remember when he blew the whistle on that factory employing and abusing illegal immigrants?

b) Simple: they offered him a bribe, he accepted it.

c) That's almost correct. In fact, I resigned last month when the media revealed they'd been involved in industrial espionage.

d) Apparently he's been sacked. He phoned in sick far too often, they say.

e) Well done. I can't say that much. I phoned home every single day last week when my son was ill.

f) Well, a few years back he was suspected of tax evasion. That's all I know.

WRITING **A** **Cross out the incorrect linker.**

1 Cyberspace fraud is a real risk ...., the volume of Internet transactions is on the increase.

a) But   b) However   c) Still

2 .... Internet security is improving, the number of cybercrime victims remains high.

a) Although   b) Besides   c) Even though

3 They ordered goods online. The goods never arrived. ...., they soon found out that other people were fraudulently using their credit card number!

a) Therefore   b) Besides   c) In addition

4 A trustworthy online seller will give you all the details about the products or services. ...., they will also provide information about refunds and cancellations.

a) Furthermore   b) Even though   c) Besides

5 Many pseudo-companies use the Internet for dishonest 'business'. ...., consumer protection agencies receive thousands of complaints.

a) As a result   b) Consequently   c) Owing to

6 .... the large number of complaints our agency receives, we are unable to answer all of them personally.

a) In view of   b) Owing to   c) Consequently

7 History has shown that monopolies do not pass savings on to customers and .... do not have the proper incentive to innovate due to lack of competition.

a) in addition   b) as a result   c) furthermore

B **Put the sentences (a–g) in the correct order to write an e-mail.**

From:	Paul Edwards
To:	All staff
Subject:	Use of work facilities

a) Besides, any increase in our overheads means a reduction in everybody's end-of-year bonus. ☐

b) Consequently, I have to remind all staff that using work facilities for private purposes is unethical. ☐

c) Two of our main customers have recently remarked that trying to get through to us on the phone has become rather difficult. ☐ 1

d) I am therefore forced to conclude that members of staff are using our phones for personal calls. ☐

e) In addition, our telephone bills have increased steadily over the past 18 months. ☐

f) This, however, has not been matched by a comparable increase in the volume of our business transactions. ☐

g) Can I urge everyone who needs to make a private call to use either the public phone in the cafeteria or their personal mobiles. ☐ 7

C **Read the passage below about Fairtrade.**

- In most of the lines **1–13** there is **one extra word** which does not fit. Some lines, however, are correct.
- If a line is **correct**, put a tick (✓) in the space provided.
- If there is an **extra word** in the line, write that word in the space.

The Fairtrade Foundation is the independent certification body that awards   1 ......✓......

the FAIRTRADE Mark to products that meet up specific standards. The Foundation   2 ......up......

describes and the Mark as 'the only independent consumer label which appears   3 ....

on products as a guarantee that disadvantaged producers are getting a better deal'.   4 ....

The standards which include 'a fair and stable price' paid to farmers for their   5 ....

products and a strict environmental standards. In the UK, one in four bananas sold is   6 ....

Fairtrade certified. The list of products in certified by the Foundation is growing and   7 ....

as well as coffee, tea, chocolate and bananas, it now includes the beauty products and   8 ....

cotton. All the major British supermarket chains they now stock Fairtrade products.   9 ....

Besides it, multinational companies such as Kraft have already launched products   10 ....

advertised as 'ethically sourced'.

Leadership

VOCABULARY   **A**   **Complete the sentences with the words from the box.**

~~decisive~~	approachable	radical	encouraging	diffident	realistic

1 What they need is a ...... *decisive* ...... person, someone who can choose the right course of action even in a very difficult situation.

2 What I like about our new boss is his .... attitude. He's so good at giving us support and confidence.

3 As a team leader, Marta was extremely .... She always seemed to know what goals we would be able to achieve and which tasks would be beyond our abilities.

4 Many people find Jim rather .... They say he rarely expresses his opinions and never shows how he feels.

5 Martin is really friendly and easy to talk to. In fact, he's the most .... boss we've ever had.

6 The new office manager has rather .... ideas. Not only does he want to change the way we work, he also wants us to think in new ways!

B   **Complete the opposites of the adjectives given.**

1 realistic   i d e a l i s t i c   5 radical   _ _ n _ _ _ v _ _ _ _ _

2 principled   _ _ t h _ _ s s   6 formal   c _ s _ _ _

3 encouraging   c r _ _ _ _ _ _   7 diffident   _ s s _ _ _ _ v _

4 approachable   _ _ s t _ _ t   8 decisive   c _ _ t _ _ _ s

C   **Complete each sentence with the correct form of a verb from the box.**

~~take~~	be	carry	come	deal
get	hand	put	stand	

1 I have too much to do already, so I can't possibly ..... *take* ..... on any extra work.

2 Over the last two years, the government's economic policies have .... in for a lot of criticism.

3 The new manager has promised to .... with the issue of gender discrimination.

4 Rick was a ruthless boss who caused several employees to .... in their resignation.

5 He had only been two weeks in the job when he realised he .... not up to it.

6 A number of controversial reform proposals were .... forward at the meeting.

LANGUAGE REVIEW

A **Cross out the incorrect relative pronoun in each of the sentences below.**

1 It is unbelievable what people *who /~~which~~* believe in themselves can accomplish.

2 The ability to motivate people is one of the greatest assets *that /who* a leader can possess.

3 Do you agree that successful people are those *who /which* seize opportunities and take risks?

4 Mandela, *that /who* is often considered to be the greatest statesman of our time, has most of the qualities *that /who* a successful leader has to have.

5 The assertiveness training workshop, *which /that* starts next month, is designed for anyone *who /which* is or will be a team leader.

6 The meetings *that /who* we hold on Friday afternoons are compulsory for everyone.

B **Complete the text with *who*, *that* or *which*.**

Carl Rogers, ...*who*...[1] is regarded as the founder of the 'person-centred approach', was one of the greatest psychologists of all time. Today, more than two decades after his death, his ideas are still at the core of many leadership training and communication skills courses. His theory, ...[2] developed over many years of experience with clients, is built on the belief that all human beings want to do the best they can, to realise their potential. Rogers identified a number of features of effective communication, the kind of communication ....[3] can help people understand and overcome whatever prevents them from fulfilling their potential.

There are three qualities ....[4] make effective communication possible.

The first, ...[5] many consider the most important one, is called 'empathy'. It is a quality ....[6] anybody ....[7] is in a position of leadership needs to have. Indeed, good leaders need to be able to see the world through the eyes of those ....[8] work with them. The second quality is 'genuineness'. A genuine person is someone ....[9] does not hide their real thoughts, feelings, or intentions.

It is this quality ....[10] enables you to be the person ....[11] you really are.

'Acceptance' is the third quality, the one ....[12] helps you respect and accept people as they are.

Good leaders, ...[13] also need to be good communicators, have to have those qualities. Many people would say that, in addition, a really good leader is one ....[14] is able to develop such qualities in others. ∎

C **In the job advertisement below, the relative pronouns are missing. Insert the pronouns into the text, where appropriate.**

Managing Director, circa €70,000 + Benefits

which (or that)

Mobirex is a leading European company ∧ provides high-quality mobile marketing and mobile content solutions. Founded in 1999, Mobirex is a fast-growing company is looking for a visionary leader can respond to the challenge of international growth. The candidate, must have at least five years' experience in the field of mobile technology, will be a highly motivated individual will provide firm strategic leadership. The successful candidate will lead a dynamic team achieved record sales last year.

LANGUAGE WORK

LANGUAGE +

> **Tip**
>
> We use *whose* in defining or non-defining relative clauses instead of *his / her / their*.
>
> We can also use *whose* instead of *its*:
>
> • Do you know the company? Its CEO was suspected of fraud.
>
> → Do you know the company **whose** CEO was suspected of fraud?
>
> • This is the team. We interviewed their leader last week.
>
> → This the team **whose** leader we interviewed last week.
>
> • Enzo Ferrari died in 1988. His cars achieved cult status.
>
> → Enzo Ferrari, **whose** cars achieved cult status, died in 1988.

D Combine these sentences using *whose*.

1 The CEO Anton Vizi resigned last week. His leadership style had come in for a lot of criticism.

The CEO Anton Vizi, ...

2 Some staff are disappointed. Their training programme was postponed.

The staff ....

3 Some stores will have to be closed down. Their performance is deteriorating.

The stores ....

4 United Steel is now almost bankrupt. Its former director was guilty of bribery and corruption.

United Steel, ...

E Decide whether the relative clauses in Exercise D are defining or non-defining.

1 *non-defining*   3 ....

2 ....   4 ....

WRITING

A Complete the e-mail with the correct form of the verbs from the box.

confirm	attend	contact	discuss	do
like	make	see	send	

From:	Gijsbert Andriessen
To:	Renata Luccarini
Date:	15 January
Subject:	Leadership training seminar

Dear Renata,

This is just to ...*confirm*...[1] that I'll arrive in Udine on 5 February and would ....[2] our introductory session to start at 10 a.m. on the 6th, as we ....[3] last week.

I was wondering if you could ....[4] me a favour. Could you please ....[5] sure that all six regional representatives are invited as soon as possible, as it is essential that they ....[6] the seminar. I have not been able to ....[7] them myself as I always seem to be on a plane or a train these days!

Please ....[8] me the full list of participants by 25 January.

Many thanks in advance.

Looking forward to ....[9] you soon,

Gijsbert

B   **Study the examples and the tips.**

Spoken or informal written English	Formal written English
Please send us the report (that / which) you referred **to**.	Please send us the report **to which** you referred.
We know the people (who) he got a recommendation **from**.	We know the people **from whom** he received a recommendation.
Could you send us the list of applicants (who) you have not been able to get in touch **with**?	Could you send us the list of applicants **with whom** you have not been able to get in touch?
We attach some information about the area (that / which) you will be responsible **for**.	We attach some information about the area **for which** you will be responsible.

Tips
- In spoken English or informal written English, we usually leave out *who / that / which* and put the preposition at the end of the relative clause.
- In formal written English, we often put the preposition in front of *which / whom*.
- We cannot use *that* after a preposition.
- After a preposition, we use the form *whom*, not *who*.

Now rewrite the following sentences in a more formal style.

1   As a leader, she motivated anyone she worked **with**.

2   The representatives we spoke **to** were very helpful.

3   The company I used to work **for** is now facing a financial crisis.

4   That is the project I'm most interested **in**.

5   The problems we have to deal **with** are rather serious.

6   Here are the details of the businesses we've invested **in**.

C   **Read the passage below about poor leadership.**

- In each line **1–10**, there is **one wrong word**.
- For each line, **underline the wrong word** in the text, and **write the correct word** in the space provided.

Poor leadership almost inevitably results in ineffective organisations. These

share a number of characteristics.

Firstly, they are weakened by interpersonal conflicts which <u>remains</u> unresolved   1   *remain*

and are allowed to get worst. Secondly, channels of communication are often   2   ....

blocked, so that information is no adequately shared: everyone has 'secrets'   3   ....

which they reveal only to theirs closest friends. In addition, there are conflicts   4   ....

of interest between individually members of staff and the organisation, which   5   ....

frequently cause huge losses for energy. Finally, staff typically feel powerless,   6   ....

cut off from a decision-making process. Consequently, hardly anyone feels   7   ....

motivated for give the best of themselves.   8   ....

Such a situation can be remedied by a leader which decides to put people first,   9   ....

to focus on team building, and to finding ways of empowering staff.   10   ....

LANGUAGE WORK

VOCABULARY   **A**   **Complete each pair of sentences with the same adjective from the box.**

cut-throat	aggressive	deep	fierce	heavy
intense	strong	tough	unfair	

1 a) The ...*cut-throat*... competition in PCs is keeping prices relatively low.

   b) Alfitel and Deltelcom are engaged in a ...*cut-throat*... battle for market share.

2 a) Sonara reduced their prices so much that they were accused of .... competition.

   b) Brent & Kay have an .... advantage over their competitors because of their connections with the Board of Trade.

3 a) There will be .... competition for the contract as the terms are excellent.

   b) At this time of the year, all fruit growers are involved in .... activity.

4 a) Everybody knows that competition to win a stake in United Telecommunications will be ....

   b) Deliveries were delayed owing to .... storms in the north of the country.

5 a) European mobile phone manufacturers are under .... price competition from Korean companies.

   b) A good leader has to be able to make .... decisions when necessary, and to make them quickly.

6 a) Prices have gone down owing to .... competition.

   b) The CEO says the .... pound is responsible for the fall in exports.

B   **Complete the sentences with words from the box. You will not need all the words, and you may use the same word more than once.**

across	against	for	off	over	to	up	with

1 Lowering our prices would be a rather ineffective way of responding ...*to*... the competition.

2 Many corner shops were unable to cope .... the competition from supermarkets and had to close down.

3 If they invest in mobile phone technology, they stand a good chance of catching .... their competitors.

4 Some businesses are finding it difficult to adapt .... such a volatile market.

5 Local clothes manufacturers can no longer fight .... the competition from global brands.

6 If you opened a computer retail shop in our city, you would be .... very strong competition.

C **Correct the two sentences in which the idiom from sport is used incorrectly.**

1 Although she is past normal retirement age, she is obviously still in the driving seat of the company.

2 The market keeps changing all the time, so you have to stay alert and keep your eye on the ball.

3 With Alfitel years ahead of their competitors, many people say it is now a one race horse.

4 In our country, Nokia and Ericsson are neck and neck. They are both equally successful.

5 Now they want to extend the deadline and renegotiate the terms and conditions. We'll never reach an agreement if they keep changing the goalkeepers.

VOCABULARY +

D **Match these idioms from sport with their definition.**

1 to pull one's punches
2 to kick off
3 the ball is in your court
4 to sink or swim
5 to backpedal
6 to be thrown in at the deep end

a) it is your turn to take action
b) to be given something difficult to do without any help
c) to act or fight with less force than you could
d) to go back on a promise
e) to succeed or to fail without help from anybody else
f) to start (an event, a discussion, etc.)

E **Complete the sentences with the appropriate form of an idiom from Exercise D.**

1 If we want to remain the market leader, we need to be more aggressive. We can't afford to ...*pull our punches*....

2 In the current climate of fierce competition, start-up companies just have to ....

3 United Software will .... their massive advertising campaign in May.

4 We have made Banque du Commerce the best possible offer. So let's wait and see now – ....

5 Young entrepreneurs often feel that they .... They have everything to learn and do not often get much help.

6 We thought they were going to keep their promises this time but once again they .... on their commitments at the last minute.

LANGUAGE REVIEW

A **The passive sentences below are all possible grammatically, but three are rather unnatural. Put a cross next to the sentences you think seem unnatural and rewrite them so that they sound more natural.**

1 All their necklaces and bracelets are made in India. ☐

2 We were written to by someone enquiring about our jewellery products. ☐

3 Our latest designs are aimed at fashion-conscious men and women. ☐

4 The results of the survey were published in a business magazine. ☐

5 Unfortunately, some complaints were received by us about our new design. ☐

6 We are glad to confirm that your company will be visited by members of our buying department. ☐

B Complete each sentence with a passive form of the verbs in the box.

~~create~~	test	award	invent	reward	make	modify

1 New designs *are being created* all the time.

2 Last year, the special prize .... to two young entrepreneurs.

3 The new clothes will .... from a fibre that reflects light.

4 The light bulb .... by Edison.

5 The design .... already .... twice because of poor test results.

6 In my opinion, originality and imagination should .... more highly than just hard work.

7 All new medicines must eventually .... on humans.

C Make these sentences passive. Only use *by* if it is important to say who performed the action.

1 They manufacture all our new models in Mumbai.

All our new models are manufactured in Mumbai.

2 The Artisans Co-operative is developing a new range of jewellery.

3 Rashid Singh Enterprises will make the earrings.

4 I think we should discontinue this range of products immediately.

5 Scientists were testing the new drugs.

6 We have reduced the number of subsidiaries dramatically.

7 The CEO evaluated the marketers' ideas regularly.

8 Our engineers could make some modifications.

LANGUAGE +

D Study the examples and the rule. Then change the sentences below in the same way.

- We should ask someone to redesign our website for us.
  We should have our website redesigned.

- We didn't pack these products ourselves.
  We had these products packed.

What's the rule?

- We use *have something done* (*have* + object + past participle) when we arrange for someone else to do some work for us.
- In informal spoken English, we can use *get* instead of *have*. For example: *We must get this report published.*

1 We will ask someone to translate the specifications.
..*We will have the specifications translated.*..

2 We won't train the representatives ourselves.
....

3 We assemble the machines but we ask other people to make the components for us.
....

4 We are not building a new laboratory ourselves.
....

5 Someone has analysed all the data for us.
....

6 We haven't delivered our new catalogue to all our customers ourselves.
....

LANGUAGE WORK

WRITING **A** **Rewrite this informal e-mail, replacing the phrases in *italics* with passives.**

From:	lankford25@eircom.net
To:	ralf.bublitz@nourel.de
Subject:	Your order No. B/022/N

Dear Mr Bublitz

Thank you for your order. We are pleased to advise you that *we are now processing it. We will pack each item* individually in accordance with your instructions. *We have already made arrangements for shipment to Bonn*, and *we will despatch the goods* within ten days.

Meanwhile, we would like to inform you that *you can access our new catalogue* at www.lankford.com.

Yours sincerely

Maureen Doyle
Sales Manager

From:	lankford25@eircom.net
To:	ralf.bublitz@nourel.de
Subject:	Your order No. B/022/N

Dear Mr Bublitz

Thank you for your order. We are pleased to advise you that *it is being processed.*

....
....
....
....
....

Yours sincerely

Maureen Doyle
Sales Manager

Tip
We choose passive forms if we want our writing to be more formal.

B **Match these sentence halves.**

i In addition, follow-up meetings with

ii This report was commissioned

iii The strategy was developed following

iv The report was to be submitted

v It describes a two-pronged strategy for

a) by March 30, together with recommendations for action.

b) repositioning the two travel agencies recently acquired by Intex Inc.

c) a very detailed study.

d) by Mr Don Chapman, Chief Executive of Intex Inc.

e) all major stakeholders also contributed to the concept.

C **Reorder the sentences in Exercise B to make the introductory section of a report.**

1 [ii]   2 [ ]   3 [ ]   4 [ ]   5 [ ]

D **Read the text below about unfair competition.**

- In each line **1–9**, there is **one wrong word**.
- For each line, **underline the wrong word** in the text, and **write the correct word** in the space provided.

Every year, trade ministers from over 100 countries meet within a framework	1 ....*the*............
of the WTO for discuss reform of world trade rules.	2 ....
Critics argue that the organisation needs to do many more to make trade fair,	3 ....
particularly in two areas. Firstly, rich members of the WTO must reducing	4 ....
agricultural subsidies paid for their farmers, as this leads to surplus produce	5 ....
being dumped onto poorer countries. In turn, this export dumping destroy the	6 ....
livelihoods of million of poor farmers. Secondly, the WTO must stop forcing	7 ....
developing countries to open their markets complete, as those countries	8 ....
obviously need to protect fragile industries in the face of unfairly competition.	9 ....

Talk business

The aim of this *Talk business* section is to make you more aware of some of the main features of English pronunciation. This will help you understand spoken English more easily. Hopefully, it will also help you discover areas you may need to work on for your spoken English to sound more natural.

◀》 **1 Look, listen and repeat.**

Vowel sounds

/ɪ/   quick fix
/iː/   clean sheet
/e/   sell well
/æ/   bad bank
/ɑː/   smart card
/ɒ/   top job
/ɔː/   short course
/ʊ/   good books
/uː/   school rules
/ʌ/   much luck
/ɜː/   first term
/ə/   a'bout 'Canada

Diphthongs

/eɪ/ play safe
/aɪ/ my price
/ɔɪ/ choice oil
/aʊ/ downtown
/əʊ/ go slow
/ɪə/ near here
/eə/ fair share

Consonants

1 Contrasting voiceless and voiced consonants

Voiceless		Voiced	
/p/	pay	/b/	buy
/f/	file	/v/	value
/t/	tax	/d/	deal
/θ/	think	/ð/	this
/tʃ/	cheap	/dʒ/	job
/s/	sell	/z/	zero
/k/	card	/g/	gain
/ʃ/	option	/ʒ/	decision

2 Other consonants

/m/	mine	/n/	net	/ŋ/	branding	/h/	high
/l/	loss	/r/	rise	/w/	win	/j/	year

Tips

* Identify the sounds that you have difficulty recognising or producing and focus mainly on these.
* Add your own key words in the tables above for the sounds you wish to focus on.
* Using the pause button on your CD player will give you time to speak or write when you do the exercises.

USING A DICTIONARY

Any good dictionary today gives you useful information on the pronunciation of individual words. With the help of the *Longman Business English Dictionary* or the *Longman Wordwise Dictionary*, for example, you will be able to work out the pronunciation of any English word on your own once you are familiar with the phonetic symbols above.
In addition, the dictionary also gives you essential information about *word stress*. When a word has more than one syllable, we always put more stress on one of the syllables, i.e., we speak that syllable more strongly. Look at the dictionary entry for *compete*:

com·pete /kəmˈpiːt/ *v* [I] to try to win something or to be more successful than someone else:

- The ˈ sign shows you that the syllable immediately after it should be stressed: comPETE. You will find various exercises on word stress in Units 4, 8, 11 and 12.

- The : sign shows you that the vowel is long. The contrast between *long* and *short* vowels is very important for mutual understanding. In Unit 1, for example, you will find an exercise on /ɪ/ and /iː/.

SOUNDS AND SPELLING

In English,
a) the same sound can be spelt in different ways,
b) the same letters can be pronounced in different ways.
a) Consider for example /əʊ/, the sound of *go slow*. It can be spelt *o* as in **o**pen, *oa* as in l**oa**n, *oe* as in t**oe**, *ough* as in alth**ough**, *ow* as in kn**ow**, or *eou* as in S**eou**l.
b) Take the letter *u* for instance. It can be pronounced /ʌ/ as in c**u**t, /ʊ/ as in f**u**ll, /ɜː/ as in t**u**rn, /ɔː/ as in s**u**re, /juː/ as in t**u**ne, or /ɪ/ as in b**u**sy.

Put the following words under the correct sound in the table below (the letters in bold show the sound).

break	Europe	insurance	advice	train
buyer	friendship	knowledge	said	want
chair	heart	laugh	scientific	their
conscious		million		height

Vowels		
/ɒ/	/e/	/ɑː/
1 job	1 sell	1 card
2	2	2 ....
3	3	3 ....

/eɪ/	/eə/	/aɪ/
1 pay	1 share	1 price
2	2	2 ....
3	3	3 ....

Consonants		
/ʃ/	/s/	/j/
1 option	1 sell	1 year
2	2	2 ....
3	3	3 ....

Sound–spelling relationships are explored in Unit 8, for example.

SHADOWING

Shadowing is a very effective way to make the most of the recorded material.
1   Play a short section, i.e. a few words or one line of a dialogue, then pause.
2   Without speaking, repeat internally what you heard.
3   Play the same section again. Pause and speak the words in exactly the same way and at the same speed. Repeat this step until you are completely satisfied with your performance.
4   Play the same section again and speak along with the voice on the recording. This is shadowing.
5   Move on to the next short section of the recording and repeat the same procedure.

Brands

SOUND WORK

INDIVIDUAL SOUNDS

A Put the words from the box into the correct column, according to the pronunciation of the letter(s) in bold.

app**ea**l	bel**ie**ve	bus**i**ness	**i**mage
incr**ea**singly	man**a**gement	p**eo**ple	w**o**men

/ɪ/ as in qu**i**ck f**i**x

....

....

....

....

/iː/ as in cl**ea**n sh**ee**t

..... *appeal* .....

....

....

....

🔊 2 **Check your answers. Then listen and practise saying the words.**

B 🔊 3 **Listen to how these verb forms are pronounced.**

sell	sells	be·lieve	be·lieves
launch	laun·ches	pro·duce	pro·du·ces
cost	costs	de·ve·lop	de·ve·lops
use	u·ses	es·ta·blish	es·ta·bli·shes

(Note: The symbol · is used to separate the syllables in the words.)

What's the rule?

If the infinitive ends in /s/, /z/, /ʃ/, /ʒ/, /tʃ/ or /dʒ/, the third person singular ending of the present simple is pronounced /ɪz/, and the word gets an extra syllable.

C Underline the forms which are one syllable longer than the infinitive. Check your answers.

1	create	creates	6	face	faces
2	focus	<u>focuses</u>	7	suggest	suggests
3	design	designs	8	increase	increases
4	raise	raises	9	generate	generates
5	advertise	advertises	10	endorse	endorses

🔊 4 **Now listen and practise saying the pairs of verb forms.**

CONNECTED SPEECH

D 🔊 5 **Listen to the recording and complete the sentences with the contracted forms that you hear.**

1 Think about our clients. ...... *They're* ...... looking for something that'll make their brand more exciting.

2 .... doing a lot of advertising to establish our brand.

3 I just .... think we should increase our prices.

4 Well, ... not sure .... a good idea to stop manufacturing in Europe.

5 Why .... we change our pricing policy?

6 Let's get in touch with Sandra and see if .... interested.

MAKING SUGGESTIONS

A Complete Speaker A's suggestions with an appropriate phrase from the box.

How about	How do you feel	In my view
I suggest that	I think we	Why don't we

Speaker A's suggestions

1 .....*How about*..... reducing the price by 15%?

2 .... aim our products at young people only?

3 .... should license the whole product range.

4 .... about redesigning the packaging?

5 ...., we should devise a new advertising campaign.

6 .... we try and project a new image to appeal to a different market segment.

🔊 **6 Listen to check your answers.**

B Match Speaker B's responses to Speaker A's suggestions in Exercise A.

Speaker B's responses

a) I see what you mean, but surely you know how much we already spend on TV commercials. ☑5

b) I'm afraid I can't agree. Our products are already among the cheapest on the market. ☐

c) That's a great idea! I think we're focusing on too many segments of the market. ☐

d) Yes, I'd go along with that. But what to change? The logo? The taste? ☐

e) Maybe, but bear in mind that the 'Made in Finland' label attracts a lot of customers. ☐

f) Mm, good idea. I think it looks rather boring, to be honest. ☐

🔊 **7 Listen to check your answers. Then listen again, and practise Speaker B's responses.**

GETTING THE MESSAGE RIGHT

C 🔊 **8 Listen to five different speakers and decide what each one is doing.**

• Write one letter (**a–h**) next to the number of the speaker.
• Do not use any letter more than once.

Speaker 1 ....

Speaker 2 ....

Speaker 3 ....

Speaker 4 ....

Speaker 5 ....

a) confirming arrangements
b) expressing disagreement
c) giving an invitation
d) giving instructions
e) making a complaint
f) making a suggestion
g) requesting advice
h) requesting information

SURVIVAL BUSINESS ENGLISH

SOUND WORK

INDIVIDUAL SOUNDS

A 🔊 **9 Listen and underline the word you hear.**

1	<u>wrong</u>	strong	7	rice	price
2	rain	train	8	port	sport
3	rest	stressed	9	asleep	sleep
4	asleep	sleep	10	rest	stressed
5	port	sport	11	rain	train
6	rice	price	12	wrong	strong

What's the rule?

All the words on the right have two or three consonant sounds at the beginning. When you say those words, do **not** put a vowel sound before or between the consonants.

🔊 **9 Check your answers. Then listen again and practise the sentences.**

B 🔊 **10 Listen and complete the words with the missing consonants.**

1   I'll take the high- ....*sp*.eed ....*tr*.ain.

2   There's a ....oblem with our ....ategy.

3   We're going to ....ain more ....aff.

4   We'll ....obably ....etch our ....and.

5   ....eve is ....ying to ....ankfurt on ....iday.

6   Our ....ench ....ores are ....ylish and ....acious.

🔊 **10 Check your answers. Then listen again and practise the sentences.**

CONNECTED SPEECH

C 🔊 **11 Circle the sentences (a or b) that you hear.**

1	(a) They travel by train.	b) They'll travel by train.
2	a) It cost us a lot more.	b) It'll cost us a lot more.
3	a) I'm afraid he let us down.	b) I'm afraid he'll let us down.
4	a) We visit them every Thursday.	b) We'll visit them every Thursday.
5	a) You go to Frankfurt every week.	b) You'll go to Frankfurt every week.
6	a) I leave at six.	b) I'll leave at six.

What's the rule?

Notice the pronunciation of the contracted forms such as *you'll*, *we'll*, *they'll*, etc. The / l / in those contractions is called **dark l**. It is different from the **clear l** in *luggage*, *delay*, *we'll arrive*, for example. / l / is clear before a vowel sound or / j / but dark elsewhere, as for example in *film*, *milk*, etc.

🔊 **11 Now listen again and practise the sentences.**

STRESS AND INTONATION

D 🔊 **12** In *wh-* questions, the voice usually goes down at the end. Listen to these examples.

1 What time do I have to check in?

2 Who will pick her up at the airport?

E 🔊 **13** Listen and complete these *wh-* questions. Then check your answers.

1 When will she be ....back........?

2 How much is a .... ticket?

3 Why was your train ....?

4 How long is the ....?

5 What time is the .... flight?

🔊 **13** Listen again and practise the falling intonation.

ASKING FOR AGREEMENT OR CONFIRMATION

A 🔊 **14** A question tag is a short question that we often put on the end of a sentence when we speak. Listen to the intonation in these question tags.

1 Surely there's an earlier flight, *isn't there?*

2 This queue doesn't seem to be moving, *does it?*

What's the rule?

Question tags have a different function depending on the intonation used.

- If the voice rises, as in example 1, the speaker is checking information. So this is more like a genuine question.
- If the voice falls, as in example 2, the speaker is just saying what he or she thinks.

B 🔊 **15** Listen to these question tags and tick the correct box (↗) or (↘).

	↗	↘			↗	↘
1				4		
2				5		
3				6		

🔊 **15** Now listen again and practise the sentences.

GETTING THE MESSAGE RIGHT

C 🔊 **16** Listen to five messages, and decide what each speaker wants to do.

- Write one letter (**a–h**) next to the number of the message.
- Do not use any letter more than once.

Message 1 ....

Message 2 ....

Message 3 ....

Message 4 ....

Message 5 ....

a) cancel an appointment

b) express disagreement

c) give feedback

d) give instructions

e) make a complaint

f) make a suggestion

g) make an appointment

h) request information

SOUND WORK

INDIVIDUAL SOUNDS

A 🔊 **17 Listen to the *schwa* sound (/ə/) in these words.**

a'dapted	con'verted	'customised	'second
	com'puter	con'siderably	'February

> **Tip**
> The *schwa* sound (/ə/) is very frequent in English. Notice that non-stressed syllables often have /ə/.

🔊 **17 Listen to the words again and practise saying them.**

B 🔊 **18 Listen and underline *all* the *schwa* sounds that can you hear. Then check your answers.**

1 We've converted the station into a hotel.

2 They've adapted the equipment.

3 They've customised the computer programs.

4 They've had second thoughts about the project.

5 Things have improved considerably since January.

🔊 **18 Now listen again. Practise saying each sentence after you hear it.**

CONNECTED SPEECH

C 🔊 **19 Listen to the pronunciation of *has / have* and *hasn't / haven't* in the following sentences.**

1 She's restructured the company.
/ʃiːz/

2 They've just relocated.
/ðeiv/

3 He hasn't retrained.
/hiˈhæznt/

4 We haven't relaunched it yet.
/wiˈhævnt/

5 Where's he gone?
/ˈweəzɪ/

6 What've they done?
/ˈwɒtəvðei/

D 🔊 **20 Listen to the recording and complete the sentences. Use contracted forms.**

1 .... changed enormously.

2 .... redesigned the office.

3 .... moved in the right direction.

4 .... been retrained to use the new equipment.

5 .... decentralised the decision-making process.

🔊 **20 Listen again and practise the sentences. Pay attention to the contractions.**

GETTING THE MESSAGE RIGHT

A ◀)) **21 Listen to these extracts from meetings, and decide what each speaker is doing. Each extract is spoken twice on the recording.**

- Write one letter, (**a–g**), next to the number of the speaker.
- You will have to use each letter twice.

Speaker 1 ....

Speaker 2 ....

Speaker 3 ....

Speaker 4 ....

Speaker 5 ....

Speaker 6 ....

Speaker 7 ....

Speaker 8 ....

Speaker 9 ....

Speaker 10 ....

Speaker 11 ....

Speaker 12 ....

Speaker 13 ....

Speaker 14 ....

a) starting the meeting
b) setting objectives
c) asking for reactions
d) dealing with interruptions
e) keeping to the point
f) speeding up or slowing down
g) summarising

ASKING FOR REPETITION

B ◀)) **22 Listen to how Speaker B asks for the piece of information that is underlined to be repeated. Notice how the voice keeps rising from the beginning of the question to the end.**

1 A: They complained that <u>the work schedule was too tight</u>.
   B: I'm afraid I didn't quite catch that. What did you say they complained about?

2 A: The interviews will be carried out <u>at our headquarters</u>.
   B: Sorry, where will the interviews be carried out, did you say?

3 A: The job sounded so interesting that <u>340</u> people applied for it.
   B: Sorry, I didn't get that. How many people did you say applied for the job?

C **Now ask Speaker A to repeat the underlined information in each of these conversations. Use the three examples in Exercise B as models.**

1 A: Out of the five short-listed candidates, <u>Pierre Meyer</u> seems to be the most suitable.

   B: ....

2 A: He's worked in Bulgaria <u>for three years</u>.

   B: ....

3 A: He graduated from <u>Imperial College London</u>.

   B: ....

4 A: He's training <u>staff from the ministry of finance</u>.

   B: ....

5 A: The project he's working on finishes <u>at the end of August</u>.

   B: ....

◀)) **23 Now listen to the sample answers and practise Speaker B's responses.**

SURVIVAL BUSINESS ENGLISH

UNIT 4 Organisation

A 🔊 24 **Listen to how the letter *u* is pronounced in the following words.**

budget	business	consumer	figures	full	purpose

B **Match each word on the left with the two words on the right which contain the same sound.**

1 budget
2 business
3 consumer
4 figures
5 full
6 purpose

a) survey, return
b) subsidiary, status
c) push, pull
d) minute, busy
e) distribute, introduce
f) consultant, customer

🔊 25 **Now listen to check your answers. Then listen again and practise the words.**

C 🔊 26 **Listen to the way certain words are linked in these sentences.**

1 We've got sales‿offices‿in‿over ten countries.
2 He's‿on‿a work placement‿in‿Italy.

What's the rule?

When a word ends with a **consonant** sound and the word immediately after begins with a **vowel** sound, we usually link those two words.

🔊 26 **Now listen again and practise the sentences.**

D **Indicate where similar links could be made in these sentences.**

1 We want to set up an overseas office in India.
2 Our company's organised in eight divisions.
3 In your opinion, what are the good qualities of our organisation?

🔊 27 **Check your answers. Then listen again and practise the sentences.**

E **Three-syllable words can have the following stress patterns: Ooo, oOo or ooO. Put the words in the box in the correct column.**

company	consumer	Japanese	decision	government
understand	equipment	interesting	policy	department

Ooo	oOo	ooO
company	consumer	Japanese
....	....	....
....	....	
....		

🔊 28 **Listen to check your answers.**

NETWORKING **A** **Match the phrases on the left with the appropriate response on the right.**

1 Hello, Julie. Nice to see you again.

2 I got promoted to head of department.

3 Which company do you represent?

4 Has your company been in business long?

5 Let me give you my business card.

6 I don't know much about it. What sort of company is it?

a) I work for Softel. We're in telecommunications.

b) Hi Tom. How are you?

c) Really? That's great. Congratulations!

d) Thanks. And I'll give you mine.

e) Well, we're basically a biotech company.

f) Yes, we're well established.

B 🔊 **29 Listen to the recording to complete these sentences.**

1 I ...*work in*.... the travel section.

2 .... project manager.

3 My .... quite a lot of paperwork.

4 I'm .... finding new business contacts in the Pacific Rim.

5 I'm .... staff training.

6 I spend a lot of time .... enquiries.

LISTENING PRACTICE **C** 🔊 **30 Listen and tick the best response (a, b or c) for each item that you hear.**

1 a) Sure. All of us are going.
   b) How about you?
   c) Pretty well at the moment.

2 a) Hi, Greg. Pleased to meet you.
   b) I've got a new computer too.
   c) Great! Are you still in sales?

3 a) Of course. Here's my business card.
   b) Yes. I'll fax them to you.
   c) You can contact me at our headquarters.

4 a) I don't see why not.
   b) We certainly made lots of useful contacts.
   c) Well, in fact we went to India.

5 a) Yes. She got promoted last week.
   b) Well, in fact Jane is head of HR.
   c) No. I changed my job six months ago.

6 a) I think it's organised in four divisions.
   b) Yeah. We work on very big projects.
   c) I'm in charge of over 20 people.

UNIT 5 Advertising

SOUND WORK

INDIVIDUAL SOUNDS

A 🔊 31 **Listen to the difference between /əʊ/ and /aʊ/.**

/əʊ/ as in g**o** sl**o**w	/aʊ/ as in d**ow**nt**ow**n
no	now
load	loud
a boat	about

B **Circle the word with a different vowel sound in each set.**

1	sl**o**gan	m**ou**th	p**o**ster	ph**o**ne
2	l**o**cal	sp**o**nsor	gr**ow**th	n**o**tice
3	all**ow**	**ou**tline	**ow**n	p**ow**er
4	l**o**go	radi**o**	kn**ow**	c**o**mmercial
5	**au**dience	acc**ou**nt	t**ow**n	backgr**ou**nd

🔊 32 **Listen to check your answers. Check with the key. Then listen again and practise saying the words.**

CONNECTED SPEECH

C 🔊 33 **Listen to these phrases and notice how the words are joined together.**

1 a clever‿ad
2 further‿information
3 a clear‿idea
4 prepare‿everything

What's the rule?

If a word ends in *-r* or *-re* and the next word begins with a vowel sound, the *-r* is usually pronounced to make a link. For example: *a clever ad* becomes /əˈklevərˈæd/.

D **Show where similar links could be made in these sentences.**

1 She was 'Advertiser of the Year' in 2004.
2 Their adverts were always thought-provoking.
3 Can I have your attention for a moment?
4 The picture is more interesting than the caption.
5 Our agency has hired a star athlete.

🔊 34 **Now listen and practise saying the sentences.**

STRESS AND INTONATION

E 🔊 35 **Listen to the intonation in this list.**

We advertise on radio, on television, in the papers and through mailshots.

What's the rule?

In lists, the intonation rises on each item except the last, where it falls.

F 🔊 36 **Listen and complete the following sentences.**

1 We want ads that are clever, eye-catching, ... and inspiring.
2 Our aim is to influence, to seduce and to ....
3 I'll give you some .... , outline the concept and finish with the storyboard.

🔊 36 **Now listen and practise saying the sentences. Pay attention to the intonation pattern illustrated in Exercise E.**

GIVING PRESENTATIONS

A **Below are the introductions to two different presentations, one quite formal, the other informal. Complete them with items from the box.**

And we'll finish with	~~ladies and gentlemen~~
everyone	My talk's in
Finally, we'll look at	Secondly
First of all, we'll analyse	Thank you
I'll kick off with	Thanks
I've divided my presentation into	Then

Formal presentation

Good morning, _ladies and gentlemen_ [1]. On behalf of Elgora International, I'd like to welcome you all. Let me introduce myself. My name's Sarah Evans, and I've been managing Elgora's department of international economic relations for the past six years.

.....................[2] for giving me the opportunity to talk to you today. The theme of my presentation is a comparison of the changes in consumer prices in the European Union and the United States from 1999 till today.

.....................[3] three parts. ....[4] the pattern of price inflation in the various countries under scrutiny. ....[5], we'll study the main factors responsible for the rise and fall of inflation in the two regions. ....[6] the forecast for the next two years.

Informal presentation

Hello ....[7]. I'm Rick Vandermeer. ....[8] for this opportunity to talk to you about our new products.

.....................[9] three parts. ....[10] the findings of the market research that led to the development of our new educational computer games. ....[11] we'll move on to a demo, so that you'll all have a chance to have a go. ....[12] your feedback and your ideas and suggestions for our forthcoming advertising campaign.

🔊 **37 Listen to the recording to check your answers.**

B **Whatever the topic or the style of your presentation, the golden rule is *put your audience first*. Match the items below to discover some useful tips about how you can do that.**

1 Be genuinely interested	a) to process the information.
2 Maintain	b) is appropriate in the host culture.
3 Avoid	c) if you know them.
4 Use individuals' names	d) in your audience as people.
5 Ask various kinds of	e) a good-natured attitude.
6 Give your audience time	f) sounding or looking superior.
7 Use as much eye-contact as	g) questions during the presentation.

SURVIVAL BUSINESS ENGLISH

UNIT 6 | Money

CONNECTED SPEECH

A 🔊 **38 Listen and complete the sentences.**

1 Let me just go through the figures .... you.

2 Sales stood .... two hundred thousand.

3 Profit went up .... 18 .... 21 million.

4 Production went down .... the end .... the year.

5 Profits rose 6% .... €9.3 million.

6 This year, orders .... Russia have levelled off.

> **Tip**
> When a preposition such as *for*, *at*, *of*, *from* or *to* occurs in the middle of a sentence, the weak form is usually used.
> For example: *for* becomes /fə/, at becomes /ət/, of becomes /əv/, from becomes /frəm/.
> Also, *to* usually becomes /tə/ before a consonant.

🔊 **38 Listen again to how the prepositions are pronounced. Then practise saying the sentences in the same way.**

STRESS AND INTONATION

B 🔊 **39 Listen to the way you pronounce dates and years.**

14th July	July 14th
1st May 1999	May 1st, 1999
22 April 2009	April 22, 2009

> **Tips**
> • In British English, you usually say and write the day first, followed by the month. In American English, it is usually the other way round: month first, followed by the day.
> • In American English, you do not need to say *the* before the ordinal.
> • When you write the date, you can leave out the ending *-st /-nd /-rd /-th*, e.g. 16 June.

C **Say these dates out loud.**

1 17 February
2 February 17
3 20 August 2005
4 June 30, 2010

5 23 March 1990
6 January 13, 2003
7 30 October 1999
8 3 September

🔊 **40 Listen to check your answers. Then listen again and practise saying the dates.**

SURVIVAL BUSINESS ENGLISH

USING STRESS TO CORRECT INFORMATION

A ◀)) **41 We need to be accurate when we talk about figures. When we make a mistake or there is a misunderstanding, we often use stress to put it right, as in this example.**

A: So revenues for the quarter increased 12.9 per cent.

B: Sorry, no. I said 12.5 per cent.

B **Underline the part which Speaker B will stress most to correct the misunderstandings in the following exchanges.**

1 A: Their shares have jumped to three hundred and eighty thousand yen.
   B: Well, my table here says three hundred and eighteen thousand, actually.

2 A: Last month, sales fell to nine hundred and fifty thousand.
   B: Worse than that, I'm afraid. They dropped to eight hundred and fifty thousand.

3 A: Let me just read that back to you, 232 623.
   B: 643 – 232 643.

4 A: We'll meet again on the thirtieth.
   B: Really? I thought we'd agreed on the thirteenth.

5 A: Production has increased by 2,450 units.
   B: Sorry. The exact figure is 2,650.

6 A: Did you say that Accounts is on the eighth floor?
   B: No. It's on the twelfth floor, actually.

◀)) **42 Now listen to the exchanges and practise Speaker B's replies.**

LISTENING PRACTICE

C **Study these graphs. They show the sales volumes for six different companies.**

A
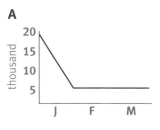

B
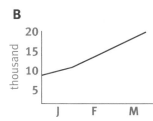

C
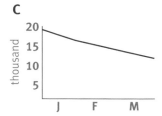

D
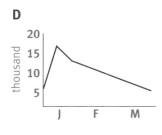

E
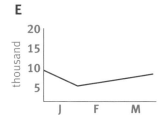

F
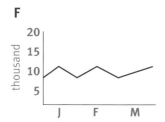

◀)) **43 Now listen to the recording, and match each description (1–6) to the appropriate graph (A–F).**

Description 1 ....   Description 4 ....

Description 2 ....   Description 5 ....

Description 3 ....   Description 6 ....

SOUND WORK

INDIVIDUAL SOUNDS

A Cross out the silent letter, i.e. the letter which is not pronounced, in each of the following words.

would	mustn't	should	foreign
know	lamb	shouldn't	listen
answer	psychology	sign	island

🔊 44 **Listen to the recording to check your answers.**

B 🔊 45 **Listen to the recording to complete the following sentences.**

1 They .... know what to say.

2 You .... show the palm of your hand.

3 You .... write them a thank-you note.

4 You .... be late for meetings.

5 You .... write anything on a business card.

🔊 45 **Now listen again and practise saying the sentences.**

CONNECTED SPEECH

C 🔊 46 **Listen to how *have to* is pronounced in these sentences.**

1 In the States, you don't have to make a lot of small talk.

2 In Brazil, you have to shake hands with everyone.

3 I'll probably have to invite them over.

4 Don't worry, you won't have to answer questions about your personal life.

What's the rule?
- *have to* is usually spoken as one word.
- It is often pronounced /ˈhæftə/ before a consonant sound (sentences 1 and 2).
- It is often pronounced /ˈhæftʊ/ before a vowel sound (sentences 3 and 4).

🔊 46 **Now listen again and practise the sentences.**

STRESS AND INTONATION

D 🔊 47 **Listen to how Speaker B highlights the word which is most significant in the context.**

1 A: Have you told anyone yet?
 B: I've told <u>Sandra</u>.

2 A: You should tell Sandra as soon as possible.
 B: I <u>have</u> told Sandra.

E **Underline the words Speaker B will highlight in these conversations.**

1 A: Do you speak any foreign languages?
 B: Well, I can speak Japanese.

2 A: What a pity you can't speak Japanese!
 B: But I can speak Japanese.

3 A: You could buy them some chocolates.
 B: I've bought them some flowers.

4 A: What about buying them some flowers?
 B: I have bought them some flowers.

🔊 48 **Listen to check your answers. Then listen again and practise Speaker B's replies.**

USING ENGLISH IN SOCIAL SITUATIONS

A Complete the conversations with the appropriate items from the box.

Excuse me	You're welcome
Congratulations	Not for me thanks
I really must get going	I'm sorry to hear that
That's a pity	I'm sorry
Never mind	It's on me

1   A: ...*Excuse me*... Do you happen to know where Agribank is?

    B: Sure. Just a bit further down the road, past the supermarket.

2   A: Have some more lamb.

    B: .... I usually eat very little meat.

3   A: Would you like to have dinner together tomorrow?

    B: .... I'm afraid we're expecting some relatives tomorrow.

4   A: Come on, stay with us a little longer.

    B: Sorry, ... It was very nice talking to you.

5   A: I've just received my MBA.

    B: ....! That's something we've got to celebrate.

6   A: Sorry, I forgot to bring back that report you lent me.

    B: .... I don't need it till next Monday.

7   A: Unfortunately, I'll probably be made redundant this winter.

    B: .... It must be a difficult situation to be in.

8   A: Let me just call the waiter.

    B: No, I'll get this. ....

◀)) **49 Listen to check your answers. Then listen again and practise Speaker B's replies.**

B   ◀)) **50 Listen to the conversations. How does the second speaker sound each time?**

> **Tip**
> Speaker B gives monosyllabic replies (i.e. the replies consist of only one syllable).
> In normal conversation, this can sound unfriendly and even rude. Speaker B should
> make it possible for the conversation to develop, for example by making a follow-up
> comment such as the examples in Exercise C.

C   ◀)) **51 Listen to Speakers 1–8 and match what they say with the responses (a–h). You will hear each speaker twice.**

a) I thought it was brilliant. You're lucky to have such an engaging speaker. ☐

b) It is, yes. But I'd wanted to come for a long time. ☐

c) Mm, yes please. That's very kind of you. ☐

d) Well, only some of the year. I spend a lot of time at head office these days. ☐

e) Very well indeed. Liz and I go back almost twenty years. ☐

f) Yeah, it's great. The restaurant is rather expensive, though. ☐

g) I'm afraid I won't be able to make it. I have to get to the airport by two. ☐

h) Yes, it's a wonderful place. I'd like to go back next year. ☐

SOUND WORK

INDIVIDUAL SOUNDS

A **Match the words in which the letters in bold are pronounced in the same way.**

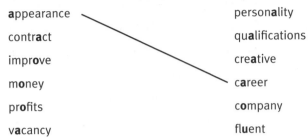

a**pp**earance   perso**n**ality

cont**ra**ct   qu**a**lifications

imp**ro**ve   cr**e**ative

m**o**ney   c**a**reer

pr**o**fits   c**o**mpany

v**a**cancy   fl**ue**nt

🔊 52 **Listen and check your answers. Then listen again and practise the words.**

CONNECTED SPEECH

B 🔊 53 **Listen to the way certain words are linked in these sentences.**

1   Tell‿us‿about your‿experience‿and qualities.
2   You'll have to liaise with‿our team‿of‿experts.

What's the rule?
When a word ends with a **consonant** sound and the word immediately after begins with a **vowel** sound, we usually link those two words.

🔊 53 **Now listen again and practise the sentences.**

C 🔊 54 **Listen and complete the sentences.**

1   I'm .... in English and Arabic.

2   I think I'm an .... planner.

3   I've .... as an adviser in an estate agency.

4   I graduated in .... from the University of Alagoas in 2006.

5   My current employer says I've got .... interpersonal skills.

6   The .... was above average but I expected a more challenging job.

🔊 54 **Listen again and indicate where links like those in Exercise B are made. Then check your answers and practise the sentences.**

STRESS AND INTONATION

D 🔊 55 **There are many words ending in *-tion*, *-ssion*, or *-sion*. Listen to the way they are pronounced.**

pro**mo**tion	dis**cu**ssion	de**ci**sion
situation	ex**pre**ssion	super**vi**sion

What's the rule?
If a word ends in *-tion*, *-ssion*, or *-sion*, the stress is always on the syllable just before the ending. Notice that *-tion* and *-ssion* are pronounced /ʃən/ and *-sion* is usually pronounced /ʒən/.

E 🔊 56 **Now listen to these words. Underline the stressed syllable.**

1   qualifications   3   conclusion   5   motivation
2   impression   4   communication   6   division

TELEPHONING

A 🔊 57 **Listen and complete the sentences.**

1 Good .... My name's Emilio Conti. ☑ M
2 I'd .... to speak to Mr Yosuke. ☐
3 Can I .... a message? ☐
4 I'm .... about your advertisement in the *Westland Echo*. ☐
5 Just one ...., please. I'll put you through. ☐
6 Hold .... ☐
7 Could you .... him to call me back tomorrow? ☐
8 I'm afraid Mr Andrade is in a .... just now. ☐
9 I was .... if you could give me a little more information. ☐
10 Good morning. How can I .... you? ☐

B **Look at items 1–10 in Exercise A. Write 'M' next to the items spoken by the person making the call, and 'R' next to those spoken by the person receiving the call.**

🔊 57 **Check your answers. Then listen again and practise.**

DICTATING AND TAKING DOWN STRANGE WORDS

C 🔊 58 **Listen and complete each column with the missing letters of the alphabet.**

/eɪ/ as in play safe	/iː/ as in clean sheet	/e/ as in sell well	/aɪ/ as in my price	/əʊ/ as in go slow	/uː/ as in school rules	/ɑː/ as in smart card
...a...	...b... ..g..	...f...	......	......	......	......
...h...	...c...	....	......		......	
......	...d...	....			......	
......	...e...	......				

Tips
• The key words will help you remember the pronunciation of each letter of the alphabet.
• When dictating or taking down a strange word, you need to know how to pronounce each letter of the alphabet clearly and accurately.

D 🔊 59 **Listen to the excerpts from phone conversations and write down the words that are spelt out.**

1 .... 5 ....
2 .... 6 ....
3 .... 7 ....
4 .... 8 ....

USING STRESS TO CORRECT INFORMATION

E **Look at these excerpts from telephone conversations. Underline the part which Speaker B will stress to correct Speaker A.**

1 A: So your office is at 36, Wellington Street.
  B: No. It's Wellington Road, in fact.
2 A: The interview is on the twenty-first, is that right?
  B: Sorry, no. It's on the twenty-third.
3 A: ... and your agent in St Petersburg is Konstantin Bupnov. B-U-P-N- ...
  B: Sorry, that's spelt B-U-B-N-O-V.
4 A: And you graduated from the University of Almeria four years ago.
  B: Well, that was five years ago, actually.

🔊 60 **Listen to check your answers. Then listen again and practise Speaker B's replies.**

SURVIVAL BUSINESS ENGLISH

International markets

INDIVIDUAL SOUNDS

A 🔊 **61 Write down the words you hear.**

1 .... 5 ....

2 .... 6 ....

3 .... 7 ....

4 .... 8 ....

What's the rule?

Some words (like **1–4**) have two consonant sounds at the end, and some other words (like **5–8**) may even have three. When you say those words, do **not** put a vowel sound between the consonants.

🔊 **61 Check your answers. Then listen again and practise the words.**

B **Complete the phrases with the words in the box.**

wants	rates	forecast	exports
exempt	employment	discount	wallets

1 belts and .... 5 tax-....................

2 needs and .... 6 self-....................

3 imports and .... 7 a sales ....

4 interest .... 8 a bulk ....

🔊 **62 Listen to check your answers. Then listen again and practise the phrases.**

C **Read the conversations and underline the groups of two or three consonant sounds at the ends of words.**

1 A: Long-term prospe<u>cts</u> are<u>n't</u> bright, are they?
  B: No. In fact, most economists forecast a slump.

2 A: Their new range of products is quite impressive.
  B: Yeah. I particularly like their sports jackets and their silk scarves.

3 A: Is it true the sales conference has been cancelled?
  B: No. It's just been postponed till the fifth of August.

4 A: So they offer a 2.5-per-cent discount for prompt payment?
  B: That's right, yes. But I don't know if their price includes insurance.

5 A: We haven't met our sales targets yet.
  B: Maybe not, but we've established excellent relationships with our agents.

6 A: To be honest, I thought our first contact was rather difficult.
  B: Well, why don't you arrange to have lunch with them next time?

🔊 **63 Check your answers. Then listen and practise the conversations.**

CONNECTED SPEECH

D ◀)) **64 Listen to how these contracted forms are spoken.**

I**'ll** try.   We**'d** refuse.
He**'ll** accept.   They**'d** agree.
She wo**n't** sign.   It **wouldn't** happen.
They wo**n't** accept.   She **wouldn't** answer.

E ◀)) **65 Listen and complete the sentences with a contracted form from Exercise D.**

1 We .... look for another supplier.

2 She .... agree to sign.

3 I .... accept their offer.

4 They .... try someone else.

5 He .... get a high discount.

6 You .... have no choice.

7 It .... arrive on time.

8 You .... have to agree.

9 It .... be difficult.

10 We .... sign.

STRESS AND INTONATION

F ◀)) **66 Listen and complete the sentences.**

1 .... you give us a more substantial discount,   we'll place a larger order. ↘

2 .... you can cover insurance,   we'll sign the deal.

3 .... you agree to split transport costs,   we won't be able to place a firm order.

4 .... you can deliver this month,   there won't be any problems.

5 .... the price is right,   we'll buy everything you produce.

◀)) **66 Listen again and practise the sentences. Notice the rising intonation on the conditional clause and the falling intonation on the main clause.**

NEGOTIATING

A ◀)) **67 Listen to five extracts from negotiations, and decide what each speaker is doing.**

• Write one letter (**a–e**) next to the number of the speaker.
• Use each letter once.

Speaker 1 ....   **a)** exploring positions

Speaker 2 ....   **b)** making a concession

Speaker 3 ....   **c)** checking understanding

Speaker 4 ....   **d)** refusing an offer

Speaker 5 ....   **e)** playing for time

SURVIVAL BUSINESS ENGLISH

SOUND WORK

INDIVIDUAL SOUNDS

A Circle the word in each line which does not contain /ʌ/, the sound in *much luck*. Then check your answers.

1	result	bonus	corruption
2	drug	company	counterfeit
3	fraud	country	month
4	business	industrial	customer
5	discuss	money	industry
6	government	unfair	supplier

◀))) **68** Listen and practise saying the words which contain /ʌ/.

CONNECTED SPEECH

B ◀))) **69** Listen to the pronunciation of *was* and *were* in these conversations.

1 A: Helen was always taking extended lunch breaks, wasn't she?
  B: Yeah, and she was phoning in sick almost every week.

2 A: What they were doing wasn't really unethical.
  B: Well, if you ask me, I'd say that it was.

3 A: The previous owners weren't exactly trustworthy.
  B: Weren't they?

4 A: Was he as corrupt as his predecessor?
  B: Yes, he was. Even more so.

5 A: Were those investments considered ethical?
  B: Of course they were.

6 A: There was a bit of a cover-up, wasn't there?
  B: There certainly was. And a major one at that.

What's the rule?

- In positive sentences *was* and *were* are usually pronounced /wəz/ and /wə/.
- At the beginning or at the end of a sentence, *was* and *were* are usually pronounced /wɒz/ and /wɜː/.
- The negative forms are usually pronounced /'wɒznt/ and /'wɜːnt/.

◀))) **69** Listen again and practise Speaker A or B's part.

STRESS AND INTONATION

C Study the examples (1–4), then complete the sentences (5–8).

Positive sentence	**Negative question tag**
1 They'd (+) already launched the new model,	hadn't (–) they?
2 They were (+) losing money,	weren't (–) they?
Negative sentence	**Positive question tag**
3 It wasn't (–) really going well,	was (+) it?
4 She hadn't (–) done anything wrong,	had (+) she?

5 He'd been discriminated against, ... he?

6 It .... a big scandal, wasn't it?

7 We weren't putting pressure on him to resign, ... we?

8 They .... bribed anyone, had they?

◀))) **70 Listen and check your answers. Notice the falling intonation on the second part of the sentence (the question tag).**

> **Tip**
>
> You can use a question tag to involve the person you are talking to in the conversation. If you simply expect the person to agree with you, your voice goes down on the tag.

◀))) **70 Listen again and practise the sentences.**

LISTENING PRACTICE

A ◀))) **71 Listen to eight extracts from discussions, and decide what each speaker is doing.**

- Write one letter (**a–d**), next to the number of the speaker.
- You will have to use each letter twice.

Speaker 1 ....

Speaker 2 ....   **a)** expressing qualified agreement

Speaker 3 ....   **b)** changing approach

Speaker 4 ....   **c)** considering possible effects

Speaker 5 ....   **d)** making a decision

Speaker 6 ....

Speaker 7 ....

Speaker 8 ....

B ◀))) **72 Listen and complete the conversation excerpts.**

1 I'm not sure I trust our new accountant. To me, all those errors seem deliberate.

   Any .... how we should address this issue? `d`

2 She's very worried about frauds with government contracts.

   .... you think we should do something about it? ☐

3 He keeps telling me that his cousin would be the best person for the job.

   What .... we do? ☐

4 Tim's already taken five days of sick leave this month.

   What do you think we .... do? ☐

5 The new office manager is putting pressure on Elaine to go out with him.

   What do you .... we do? ☐

GIVING ADVICE AND MAKING SUGGESTIONS

C **Match each request for advice in Exercise B with a suitable response.**

a) Have you thought of confronting him with the issue? He may have genuine health problems.

b) I suggest you check his personnel record first. Find out if he's ever been accused of harassment.

c) I think we should tell her not to speak to anyone. The issue's far too serious.

d) If I were you, I'd give her another chance. Honestly, she doesn't look the type of person who'd make false entries in the accounts.

e) Let's just tell him it's not on. There's no room for corruption in our company.

◀))) **73 Listen to check your answers.**

D **Underline the phrases in Exercise C used for giving advice or making suggestions.**

INDIVIDUAL SOUNDS

A Circle the word in each line which does not contain /ɜː/, the sound in *first term*. Then check your answers.

1 term	person	working	leadership
2 refer	hear	assertive	expertise
3 turn	entrepreneur	sportswear	interpret
4 energy	reserved	world	firm

◀)) 74 **Listen and practise saying the words which contain /ɜː/.**

CONNECTED SPEECH

B ◀)) 75 **Listen to the way certain words are linked in these sentences.**

1 Jim's‿awfully worried‿about‿it.
2 I don't‿agree with‿Alan‿at‿all.

What's the rule?

When a word ends with a **consonant** sound and the word immediately after begins with a **vowel** sound, we usually link those two words.

C Indicate where similar links could be made in these sentences.

1 It's the main item on our agenda.
2 First of all, could you give us the background?
3 We need more information about this issue.
4 Here are some ideas for us to think about.
5 They haven't thought about all the details.

◀)) 76 **Check your answers. Then listen and practise the sentences.**

STRESS AND INTONATION

D ◀)) 77 **Listen and underline the stressed syllable in each adjective.**

1 She was decisive, creative and highly articulate.
2 He was encouraging, dynamic and extremely idealistic.
3 She was principled, realistic and very casual.
4 He was distant, conservative and unspeakably ruthless.
5 She was cautious, humble and rather reserved.

◀)) 77 **Check your answers. Then listen again and practise the sentences.**

74

PRESENTATIONS **A** ◀)) 78 **Listen and complete these excerpts from presentations.**

1 Before I .... the next part of my talk, are there any questions on what I've said so far?

2 Good morning everyone. .... delighted .... My name's Dharamjit Singh.

3 I'm sure .... that some modifications must be made to the design.

4 If it's all right, I'll .... questions at the end of my presentation.

5 If there are no more questions, thank you again for ....

6 Thank you all for coming. Before we start, ... a few words about myself.

7 Thanks for being such .... I hope we meet again at our next convention.

LISTENING PRACTICE **B** ◀)) 79 **You will hear an excerpt from an interview with a management consultant about decision-making.**

- Before you listen, read the questions (**1–7**) below.
- As you listen, choose the best answer (**a**, **b** or **c**) for each question.
- If necessary, listen again before you check your answers.

1 According to the consultant, many people dislike making decisions because
  a) they know that doing nothing may produce better results.
  b) they are sometimes unwilling to do the best they can.
  c) they worry that their decisions may have harmful results.

2 Which of the following statements is true according to the consultant?
  a) A decision is a choice between different alternatives.
  b) Decision-making is sometimes like gambling.
  c) We can often predict the consequences of our actions accurately.

3 Why does the consultant say 'we should be grateful' when we have to make decisions? Because
  a) sometimes we do make perfect decisions.
  b) we can influence the way things happen.
  c) we stop being irresponsible.

4 What does the first step in decision-making not involve?
  a) Communicating with other people.
  b) Collecting data.
  c) Brainstorming options.

5 Why do people have to be creative and adventurous?
  a) To be prepared to cope with failure.
  b) To widen the range of options available to them.
  c) To make the right choice at the beginning.

6 What is the third step in the decision-making process called?
  a) Evaluating
  b) Listing
  c) Questioning

7 According to the consultant, the best decisions are often the ones that people make
  a) when they can speed up the process.
  b) when they can describe their guiding principles.
  c) when they make them at the right moment.

SOUND WORK

INDIVIDUAL SOUNDS

A ◀)) 80 **Listen to the difference between /ɔː/ and /əʊ/.**

/ɔː/	/əʊ/
sh**or**t c**our**se	g**o** sl**ow**
l**aw**n	l**oa**n

B ◀)) 81 **Put the words you hear into the correct column.**

	/ɔː/	/əʊ/		/ɔː/	/əʊ/
1			5		
2			6		
3			7		
4			8		

CONNECTED SPEECH

C ◀)) 82 **Listen and circle the form that you hear.**

1 They / They'll / They'd | try to dominate the market.

2 We | want to / won't / wouldn't | overtake Samsung.

3 I / I'll / I'd | listen to the news.

4 I'm sure | they / they'll / they'd | like the exhibition.

5 We know you | want to / won't / wouldn't | take the company upmarket.

6 I don't think | you / you'll / you'd | agree.

STRESS AND INTONATION

D ◀)) 83 **Listen and underline the stressed syllable in each word. Then check your answers.**

Verb	Noun (person)	Noun	Adjective
compete	competitor	competition	competitive
innovate	innovator	innovation	innovative
invent	inventor	invention	inventive
create	creator	creation	creative
protect	protector	protection	protective

◀)) 83 **Listen again and practise saying the words.**

SAYING IT TACTFULLY

A **Choose the more tactful response to each statement.**

1 Let's contact Mr Jansen next week.
   a) We should contact him earlier. b) Shouldn't we contact him earlier?

2 We'll wait till summer.
   a) That's too late. b) Isn't that too late?

Tip

Asking a negative question is an easy way to suggest or assert something tactfully.

B **Make Speaker B's responses more tactful.**

1 A: So we'll hold our next meeting in June.
   B: September would be better.

   Wouldn't .... ?

2 A: Of course, we'll order from Wilson's as usual.
   B: We should try another supplier this time.

   .... ?

3 A: They just agreed to a 10% discount for orders of 100 items or more.
   B: We could insist on better terms.

   .... ?

4 A: Let's ask Crawley Engineering for a quote.
   B: They're too expensive.

   .... ?

5 A: I think we should cancel the deal at once.
   B: We'd better wait a few more days.

   .... ?

6 A: We can deliver in 45 days, not 30 as they expect.
   B: They'll be disappointed.

   .... ?

7 A: I'll ask Mark if he wants to negotiate this contract.
   B: It would be better to ask Jenny.

   .... ?

🔊 **84 Listen to check your answers. Then listen again and practise Speaker B's responses.**

C 🔊 **85 The phrases on the left may be inappropriate in a negotiation. Listen to the recording, and complete the more tactful phrases on the right.**

1 We want thirty days' credit.   .... us thirty days' credit?

2 There's no way I can deliver in ten days.   .... deliver in ten days.

3 That's a ridiculously small order.   We were .... bigger order.

4 Credit? You must be joking!   ...., we aren't
                                                    .... to give you any credit.

5 That's impossible.   We .... to do that.

6 You've lost the contract.   .... to inform you that you
                                                    haven't won the contract.

SURVIVAL BUSINESS ENGLISH

Answer key

ANSWER KEY: LANGUAGE WORK

LANGUAGE WORK

1 Brands
Vocabulary
A

Across

2 inexpensive   4 aspirational   7 well-made
8 stylish   9 cool   11 upmarket

Down

3 value for money   5 reliable   6 timeless
8 sexy   10 fun

B

2 market
3 product
4 brand
5 product
6 market

Language review
A

2 takes
3 do / target
4 is not (isn't) working
5 Are / investing
6 works
7 are ('re) taking
8 is not (isn't) selling
9 are ('re) targeting
10 doesn't (does not) invest

B

2 manages
3 develop
4 is ('s) working
5 is ('s) supervising
6 (is) writing
7 enjoys
8 is expanding
9 has
10 owns
11 are increasing
12 is becoming

C Sample answers

2 How many new products do they develop each year?
3 Where is Ralf working this week?
4 What is he doing (in the lab)?
5 Is he writing a letter?
6 In which countries does Merlin Foods have subsidiaries?
7 Are sales and earnings for the company increasing?

D

2 believe ✓
3 belong ✓
5 consist ✓
6 contain ✓
7 depend ✓
8 prefer ✓
9 realise ✓
11 seem ✓
13 suppose ✓

E

2 Does / agree
3 does not (doesn't) contain
4 depends
5 consists
6 Do / belong

Writing
A

3 that   9 ✓
4 and   10 and
5 ✓   11 an
6 up   12 ✓
7 of   13 our
8 ✓

B Sample answer

Liz,

Following your e-mail of 10 May, I have investigated why our Sunnyvale range of products seems to be facing difficulties in Germany.

The main reason is probably due to the fact that the largest chain of supermarkets promote their own brand of soups, which they sell at a much lower price. They also usually display their own products on the top shelves, where customers can easily see them.

I also note with interest that the packaging of Vita soups, the current market leader in Germany, is almost identical to ours.

Therefore, I would like to make the following recommendations:

1) consider offering supermarket managers incentives for displaying our products properly;

2) redesign our packaging, so that it helps get across our Message '*Our foods are health foods*';

3) offer frequent discounts, especially before public holidays.

Finally, I think we should visit supermarkets and all other retail outlets much more frequently.

Jan is doing a fantastic job over there, but covering the whole of the country on his own is an impossible task. A second rep for Germany is a necessity if we do not want to lose our market share there.

With best wishes,

Stan

2 Travel

Vocabulary

A

2 legroom
3 flights
4 jet-lag
5 delays
6 cabin
7 divert

B

2 d   3 d   4 a   5 c   6 b   7 c   8 a   9 d   10 a   11 c

C

Across		Down	
3	subway	2	elevator
5	check	4	boarding
6	peak	5	car park
9	return	7	lounge
10	timetable	8	single

Language review

A

2 c   3 e   4 b   5 a

B

b 1   c 5   d 3   e 2

C

2 We're going to meet our agent to discuss our new strategy.
3 So you finish in five minutes? OK then. I'll wait for you in the lounge.
4 What time does the train arrive in Brussels?
5 By the way, Jeff, what are you doing on Thursday afternoon?
6 It's all decided now. We're (or are) going to hold the sales conference in Rome.
7 Monday morning? Just one moment. I'll just check my diary.

D

1 I'll give Mr Dupuis a ring as soon as I arrive in Brussels.
2 If my flight is delayed, I'll miss the presentation.
3 I'm going to stay here until I find a better hotel.
4 I'll visit our Chinese suppliers in May unless you advise me not to go.
5 Please come and visit our headquarters when you are in Copenhagen again.

Writing

A

2 confirm
3 As requested
4 your arrival
5 look forward to
6 sincerely

B Sample answer

I am leaving for Milan early on the morning of Friday 17th to attend a four-day seminar. I'll be back at my desk on Tuesday 8.30 a.m. as usual.

Please send out the invitations to our annual trade show on Friday morning. Also, remind Jack that I want his quarterly report on my desk when I get back.

Thanks.

3 Change

Vocabulary

A

2	update	8	reorganise
3	decentralise	9	redevelop
4	restructured	10	retrain
5	relocate	11	upgrade
6	reassess	12	deregulate
7	relaunch		

B

No change:	update; relaunch; upgrade
-ation:	decentralisation; relocation; reorganisation; deregulation
-ing:	downsizing; restructuring; retraining
-ment:	reassessment; redevelopment

C

1 reassessment
2 deregulation
3 update
4 downsizing
5 relaunch

Language review

A

2 met
3 were
4 went
5 have recovered ('ve recovered)
6 happened
7 rejected
8 looked
9 has dropped out ('s dropped out)
10 have been ('ve been)
11 have changed ('ve changed) [*changed* is also possible, especially in American English]
12 have quit ('ve quit) [*quit* is also possible, especially in American English]
13 have been ('ve been)
14 started
15 have taken up ('ve taken up)

B

The options which should be crossed out are:
2 over the last few years.
3 in 2002.
4 yet
5 last year?
6 for the past three years.

Writing

A

2 e   3 d   4 c   5 a   6 f

B

2 d   3 b   4 e   5 f   6 a

C

b 6   c 4   d 2   e 5   f 3

D

2 in order to
3 appropriate to
4 so that
5 aware of
6 decisions

E

3 ✓
4 in
5 out
6 for
7 our
8 and
9 up
10 ✓

4 Organisation

Vocabulary

A

2 b   3 d   4 c   5 a   6 a   7 a   8 c   9 b   10 d   11 d   12 c

B

2 transport
3 maintain
4 issue
5 carry out
6 train

Language review

A

2 an eighty-thousand-euro deal
3 a seven-hour journey
4 a two-million-pound loan
5 a three-day seminar
6 a sixty-storey office block

B

2 TV commercials
3 trade fair
4 information technology
5 labour force
6 research project
7 government policy

C

2 savings account
3 customs officer
4 needs analysis
5 sports car
6 labour costs

D

2 management
3 office
4 insurance
5 product
6 advertising

E

2 breach
3 conflict
4 waste
5 cost
6 range
7 round
8 lack

Writing

A

2 contribute
3 announce
4 organise
5 select
6 explain

B Sample answer

As I am a front-line employee, I believe the most useful topic for me would be 'customer service'. Although I deal well with telephone and direct enquiries, it is sometimes difficult to deal effectively with both at the same time, especially before the peak summer season.

Any advice on this would be very welcome.

C

3 ✓
4 they
5 been
6 if
7 so
8 and
9 ✓
10 the

5 Advertising

Vocabulary

A

2 c   3 a   4 b   5 c   6 c   7 a   8 b   9 a   10 b

B

to launch: b, g
to capture: c, f
to differentiate: a, e
to communicate: d, h

Language review

'Subvertising' is a combination of <u>the</u> words 'subvert' and 'advertising'. Indeed , subvertising consists of subverting or sabotaging commercial as well as political advertisements that are displayed in ⊘ public places. Here is <u>a</u> simple example: <u>an</u> advert for <u>a</u> famous brand of ⊘ cigarettes depicted <u>a</u> handsome middle-aged man gazing thoughtfully into <u>the</u> distance. <u>The</u> caption was four words long: '*The more you know...*' This ad was easily subverted by someone who just added <u>the</u> following words: '*...the less you smoke.*'

B

<u>The</u> purpose of subvertisers is usually to encourage people to think, not only about <u>the</u> products they buy, but also about <u>the</u> nature of <u>the</u> society they live in.

There are a number of similarities between advertising and subvertising: both are very often creative, witty, direct and thought-provoking.

However, <u>the</u> differences between <u>the</u> two are enormous. While <u>the</u> goal of advertising is ultimately to increase consumption and corporate profits, subvertising aims to make people aware of <u>the</u> constant pressure they are under to buy things, to spend money, to 'shop-till-you-drop', so that they may be able to resist that pressure.

C

In addition, subvertising is a reaction against <u>the</u> invasion of public places by hoardings, posters, slogans, logos, etc., which some say 'pollute our mental environment'. It is <u>an</u> attempt to 'reclaim <u>the</u> streets', to free our personal space of those consumerist messages which can be seen or heard left, right and centre in our cities.

While one cannot ignore that in <u>the</u> eyes of <u>the</u> law, altering hoardings is considered a minor form of vandalism, one has to recognise that subvertising is <u>a</u> form of creativity and <u>a</u> way of exercising one's freedom of speech.

Writing

A

2 We would be very grateful
3 we could arrange for
4 full details
5 take advantage of
6 date and time

B Sample answer

Dear Mr Costello

Thank you for your catalogue.

We are very interested in your new range of Compact copier-scanners.

We would welcome the advice of your expert as to which machines would be the most suitable for our purposes. Any day after 15:00 would be convenient, particularly Wednesday or Thursday.

We look forward to hearing from you.

Yours sincerely,

Glenda Munroe

C

2 d   3 b   4 a   5 f   6 c

D

2 <u>particularly</u> / particular
3 <u>list</u> / lists
4 <u>your</u> / you
5 <u>by</u> / for
6 <u>computers</u> / computer
7 <u>on</u> / to
8 <u>began</u> / begins

6 Money

Vocabulary

A

Across
3 revenue   5 investment   8 recession
11 forecast
Down
2 equity   4 dividend   6 stock
7 profit   9 share   10 debt

B

The verbs which should be crossed out are:
2 to work
3 to divide
4 to do
5 to pay an
6 to invoice

C

2 a   3 e   4 b   5 f   6 c

Language review

A

2 rise / fall
3 increase / decrease
4 soar / plummet
5 double / halve

C

3 drop (I)*
4 decline (I)*
5 halve (I) / (T)
6 increase (I) / (T)
7 level off (I)
8 peak (I)
9 plummet (I)
10 soar (I)

* *drop* and *decline* are also transitive in some of their senses, e.g. I dropped my reading glasses and broke them; They declined our invitation (= They refused to accept it.).

D

2 dramatically
3 gradually
4 sharply
5 significantly
6 slightly
7 steadily
8 substantially

E

1 Exports have fallen dramatically.
2 It seems that taxes are going to rise substantially.
3 The number of people out of work rose steadily.
4 Are you saying that production is declining significantly?
5 I think there will be a slight fall in domestic demand.
6 There was a gradual growth in profit.
7 There has been a sharp drop in orders.

Writing

A

2 d   3 b   4 a   5 c

B

2 however
3 despite
4 so
5 because
6 Despite
7 so
8 Although
9 However
10 although

C

2 to
3 ✔
4 ✔
5 and
6 one
7 kind
8 a
9 well
10 not
11 ✔

7 Cultures

Vocabulary

A

1 eye
2 break
3 foot
4 deep
5 on

B

1 to get into hot water
2 to be a real eye-opener
3 to feel like a fish out of water

C

1 was a real eye-opener for me
2 will ('ll) get into hot water
3 felt like a fish out of water

D

2 in
3 with
4 of
5 over
6 up

E

2 d   3 a   4 f   5 c   6 e

Language review

A

2 f   3 a   4 e   5 c   6 d

B

1 Sentences 2 and 6
2 Sentence 4
3 Sentence 5
4 Sentence 1
5 Sentence 3

C

2 have to
3 mustn't
4 don't have to
5 mustn't
6 have to
7 don't have to
8 mustn't

D

2 You mustn't drive without your seat belt on.
3 If you are invited for dinner, you should buy your hosts some flowers.
4 In many countries, you shouldn't point your finger at people.
5 Although I know them all very well, I have to address my colleagues by their surname.
6 All visitors must wear their name badge at all times.
7 Do I have to buy my hosts an expensive gift?
8 In Canada, you mustn't smoke in most public spaces.

Writing

A

a 5, 1, 7, 10, 4
b 6, 3, 2, 9, 8

B

2 I would be delighted
3 As you probably know
4 owing to previous engagements
5 as you suggested
6 if you could let me know
7 convenient for you
8 I look forward to

C

3 ✔
4 and
5 it
6 that
7 ✔
8 in
9 our
10 they
11 about

8 Human resources

Vocabulary

A

2 a headhunter
3 a probationary period
4 applicant
5 shortlist
6 a covering letter
7 a vacancy
8 a reference
9 permanent
10 interview

B

The verbs which should be crossed out are:
2 to shortlist
3 to advertise
4 to fill up
5 to work
6 to submit

Language review

A

2 c   3 f   4 a   5 b   6 e

B

1 to advertise
2 advertising
3 to advertise
4 to advertise
5 advertising

C

1 ... I suggested hiring ...
4 ... I must remember to call ...

D

1 The unions were threatening to take industrial action.
2 They offered to raise my salary by two per cent.
3 I've told my line manager I expect to be promoted next year.
4 I thought the interviewer tended to favour younger candidates.
5 I'm worried that my company intends to relocate.
6 The union claims to represent over sixty per cent of our workforce.

E

1 to
2 before
3 of
4 to
5 of

Writing

A

2 well-qualified
3 responsible to
4 successful applicant
5 fluent
6 remuneration
7 CV
8 applications
9 short-listed candidates
10 an interview

B

2 h   3 g   4 b   5 f   6 d   7 c   8 e

C

for / on
than / then
there / their
devastatingly / devastating
sometime / sometimes
closed / close
effect / effects
luckiest / luckier

9 International markets

Vocabulary

A

Across
2 dumping   4 borders   7 quotas
8 tariffs   9 controls
Down
1 subsidise   2 deregulation   3 free trade
5 customs   6 import

B

2 protected
3 quoted
4 regulations
5 meet
6 market
7 carry out

Language review

A

2 j   3 e   4 f   5 b   6 a   7 h   8 g   9 d   10 i

B

2 wouldn't
3 'll
4 won't
5 'll
6 wouldn't
7 won't
8 'd

C

2 As long as
3 Provided that
4 unless
5 in case
6 unless

ANSWER KEY

Writing

A

2 f   3 c   4 e   5 d   6 g   7 b

B

1 The date is not correct as the order was sent on *26 May.*

2 The salutation is inappropriate. It should read *Dear Mr Lambert.*

3 ... *dispatch within the next three months*, L'Illimani wants delivery within the next six weeks, so dispatch should not be within the next three months.

4 ... *sent to your bank as you requested*, L'Illimani specified that the documents and the invoice should be sent to them direct.

5 The complimentary close is inappropriate. If you use *Dear Mr /Mrs /Miss /Ms +* surname in the salutation, you should use *Yours sincerely* in the complimentary close.

C

2 a
3 ✔
4 and
5 ✔
6 more
7 have
8 for
9 very
10 to

10 Ethics

Vocabulary

A

2 testing
3 fixing
4 pollution
5 discrimination
6 espionage
7 laundering
8 counterfeit
9 fraud
10 trading

B

2 a   3 b   4 c   5 a   6 a   7 c   8 b   9 c   10 a

Language review

A

2 had always wanted
3 had been
4 had been
5 had gained
6 was
7 had applied
8 prided
9 reflected
10 had always cherished
11 were going
12 landed

13 did not know
14 contained
15 read
16 discovered
17 was
18 had already tested
19 read
20 had called
21 had informed
22 was planning (*or* planned)
23 had not experienced
24 blew
25 kept

B

2 d   3 b   4 a   5 e   6 c

Writing

A

The linkers which should be crossed out are:
2 Besides
3 Therefore
4 Even though
5 Owing to
6 Consequently
7 as a result

B

2 e   3 f   4 d   5 b   6 a

C

3 and
4 ✔
5 which
6 a
7 in
8 the
9 they
10 it

11 Leadership

Vocabulary

A

2 encouraging
3 realistic
4 diffident
5 approachable
6 radical

B

2 ruthless
3 critical
4 distant
5 conservative
6 casual
7 assertive
8 cautious

ANSWER KEY: LANGUAGE WORK

C

2 come
3 deal
4 hand
5 was
6 put

Language review

A

The correct pronouns are:
2 that
3 who
4 who / that
5 which / who
6 that

B

2 which
3 which (*or* that)
4 that (*or* which)
5 which
6 which (*or* that)
7 who (*or* that)
8 who (*or* that)
9 who (*or* that)
10 that (*or* which)
11 who (*or* that)
12 which (*or* that)
13 who
14 who (*or* that)

C

Mobirex is a leading European company **which** (or **that**) provides high-quality mobile marketing and mobile content solutions. Founded in 1999, Mobirex is a fast-growing company **which** (or **that**) is looking for a visionary leader **who** can respond to the challenge of international growth. The candidate, **who** must have at least five years' experience in the field of mobile technology, will be a highly motivated individual **who** will provide firm strategic leadership. The successful candidate will lead a dynamic team **which** (or **that**) achieved record sales last year.

D

1 The CEO Anton Vizi, whose leadership style had come in for a lot of criticism, resigned last week.
2 The staff whose training programme was postponed are disappointed.
3 The stores whose performance is deteriorating will have to be closed down.
4 United Steel, whose former director was guilty of bribery and corruption, is now almost bankrupt.

E

2 defining
3 defining
4 non-defining

Writing

A

2 like
3 discussed
4 do
5 make
6 attend
7 contact
8 send
9 seeing

B

1 As a leader, she motivated anyone with whom she worked.
2 The representatives to whom we spoke were very helpful.
3 The company for which I used to work is now facing a financial crisis.
4 That is the project in which I am most interested.
5 The problems with which we have to deal are rather serious.
6 Here are the details of the businesses in which we have invested.

C

2 <u>worst</u> / worse
3 <u>no</u> / not
4 <u>theirs</u> / their
5 <u>individually</u> / individual
6 <u>for</u> / of
7 <u>a</u> / the
8 <u>for</u> / to
9 <u>which</u> / who
10 <u>finding</u> / find

12 Competition

Vocabulary

A

2 unfair
3 intense
4 fierce
5 tough
6 strong

B

2 with
3 up with
4 to
5 off (*or* against)
6 up against

C

3 ... many people say it is now a one ~~race horse~~ horse race.
5 ... if they keep ~~changing the goalkeepers~~ moving the goalposts.

D

2 f   3 a   4 e   5 d   6 b

E

2 sink or swim
3 kick off
4 the ball is in their court
5 are thrown in at the deep end
6 backpedalled

Language review

A

2 Someone wrote to us enquiring about our jewellery products.
5 Unfortunately, we received some complaints about our new design.
6 We are glad to confirm that members of our buying department will visit your company.

B

2 was awarded
3 be made
4 was invented
5 has (already) been modified
6 be rewarded
7 be tested

C Sample answers

2 A new range of jewellery is being developed by the Artisans Co-operative.
3 The earrings will be made by Rashid Singh Enterprises.
4 I think this range of products should be discontinued immediately.
5 The new drugs were being tested (by scientists).
6 The number of subsidiaries has been dramatically reduced.
7 The marketers' ideas were regularly evaluated by the CEO.
8 Some modifications could be made (by our engineers).

D

2 We'll have the representatives trained.
3 We assemble the machines, but we have the components made.
4 We are having a new laboratory built.
5 We have had all the data analysed.
6 We have had our new catalogue delivered to all our customers.

Writing

A

Thank you for your order. We are pleased to advise you that *it is being processed. Each item will be packed* individually in accordance with your instructions. *Arrangements for shipment to Bonn have already been made*, and *the goods will be despatched within ten days*. Meanwhile, we would like to inform you that *our new catalogue can be accessed* at www.lankford.com.

B

i e   ii d   iii c   iv a   v b

C

2 v   3 iii   4 i   5 iv

D

2 <u>for</u> / to
3 <u>many</u> / much
4 <u>reducing</u> / reduce
5 <u>for</u> / to
6 <u>destroy</u> / destroys
7 <u>million</u> / millions
8 <u>complete</u> / completely
9 <u>unfairly</u> / unfair

TALK BUSINESS

Introduction

Vowels					
/ɒ/		/e/		/aː/	
1	job	1	sell	1	card
2	knowledge	2	friendship	2	heart
3	want	3	said	3	laugh
/eɪ/		/eə/		/aɪ/	
1	pay	1	share	1	price
2	break	2	chair	2	buyer
3	train	3	their	3	height
Consonants					
/ʃ/		/s/		/j/	
1	option	1	sell	1	year
2	conscious	2	advice	2	Europe
3	insurance	3	scientific	3	million

1 Brands

Sound work

A *See audio script 2.*

C *See audio script 4.*

D *See audio script 5.*

Survival business English

A *See audio script 6.*

B *See audio script 7.*

C

Speaker 1: a
Speaker 2: f
Speaker 3: h
Speaker 4: d
Speaker 5: g

2 Travel

Sound work

A *See audio script 9.*

B *See audio script 10.*

C *See audio script 11.*

E *See audio script 13.*

Survival business English

B *See audio script 15.*

C

Message 1: g
Message 2: c
Message 3: a
Message 4: e
Message 5: h

3 Change

Sound work

B *See audio script 18.*

D *See audio script 20.*

Survival business English

A

Speaker 1: c   Speaker 8: f
Speaker 2: b   Speaker 9: g
Speaker 3: a   Speaker 10: a
Speaker 4: f   Speaker 11: c
Speaker 5: g   Speaker 12: d
Speaker 6: e   Speaker 13: e
Speaker 7: d   Speaker 14: b

C *See audio script 23 for sample answers.*

4 Organisation

Sound work

B

2 d   3 e   4 b   5 c   6 a

D *See audio script 27.*

E *See audio script 28.*

Survival business English

A

2 c   3 a   4 f   5 d   6 e

B *See audio script 29.*

C

1 c   2 a   3 b   4 b   5 c   6 b

5 Advertising

Sound work

B

1 m**ou**th (as in d**ow**nt**ow**n)
2 sp**o**nsor (as in t**o**p j**o**b)
3 **ow**n (as in g**o** sl**ow**)
4 c**o**mmercial (as in **a**'bout 'Can**a**da)
5 **au**dience (as in sh**or**t c**our**se)

D *See audio script 34.*

F *See audio script 36.*

Survival business English

A *See audio script 37.*

B

2 e   3 f   4 c   5 g   6 a   7 b

6 Money

Sound work

A *See audio script 38.*

C *See audio script 40.*

Survival business English

B *See audio script 42.*

C

1 A   2 E   3 F   4 D   5 B   6 C

7 Cultures

Sound work

A *See audio script 44.*

B *See audio script 45.*

E *See audio script 48.*

Survival business English

A *See audio script 49.*

C

Speaker 1: d
Speaker 2: c
Speaker 3: a
Speaker 4: g
Speaker 5: h
Speaker 6: b
Speaker 7: f
Speaker 8: e

8 Human resources

Sound work

A *See audio script 52.*

C *See audio script 54.*

E *See audio script 56.*

Survival business English

A *See audio script 57.*

B 2 M 3 M 4 M 5 R 6 R 7 M 8 R 9 M 10 R

C *See audio script 58.*

D *See audio script 59.*

E *See audio script 60.*

9 International markets

Sound work

A *See audio script 61.*

B *See audio script 62.*

C *See audio script 63.*

E *See audio script 65.*

F *See audio script 66.*

Survival business English

A

1 d   2 e   3 b   4 c   5 a

10 Ethics

Sound work

A

The following words do not contain /ʌ/, the sound in *much luck*:

1 bonus   2 counterfeit   3 fraud
4 business   5 industry   6 supplier

C *See audio script 70.*

Survival business English

A

Speaker 1: d
Speaker 2: c
Speaker 3: b
Speaker 4: d
Speaker 5: a
Speaker 6: a
Speaker 7: c
Speaker 8: b

B *See audio script 72.*

C

2 c   3 e   4 a   5 b

D

Phrases used for giving advice or making suggestions:
a) *Have you thought of* + verb *-ing*
b) *I suggest (that) you* + infinitive without *to*
c) *I think we should* + infinitive without *to*
d) *If I were you, I'd* + infinitive without *to*
e) *Let's* + infinitive without *to*

11 Leadership

Sound work

A

The following words do not contain /ɜː/, the sound in *first term*:
1   leadership
2   hear
3   sportswear
4   energy

C *See audio script 76.*

D *See audio script 77.*

Survival business English

A *See audio script 78.*

B

1 c   2 a   3 b   4 c   5 b   6 a   7 c

12 Competition

Sound work

B

	/ɔː/	/əʊ/
1	call	
2	cause	
3		cope
4	drawn	
5		focus
6	horse	
7		goal
8	store	

C *See audio script 82.*

D *See audio script 83.*

Survival business English

A

1 b   2 b

B *See audio script 84.*

C *See audio script 85.*

The following alternative answers are also tactful:
1   Can you give us thirty days' credit?
2   I really can't deliver in ten days.
3   We were hoping for a bigger order.
4   Sorry, we aren't able to give you any credit.
5   We aren't able to do that.
6   I regret to have to inform you that you haven't won the contract.

Audio scripts

Introduction

1

The sounds of English
Vowel sounds
/ɪ/	quick fix	/ɔː/	short course
/iː/	clean sheet	/ʊ/	good books
/e/	sell well	/uː/	school rules
/æ/	bad bank	/ʌ/	much luck
/ɑː/	smart card	/ɜː/	first term
/ɒ/	top job	/ə/	a'bout 'Canada

Diphthongs
/eɪ/	play safe	/əʊ/	go slow
/aɪ/	my price	/ɪə/	near here
/ɔɪ/	choice oil	/eə/	fair share
/aʊ/	downtown		

Consonants
1 Contrasting voiceless and voiced consonants
Voiceless		Voiced	
/p/	pay	/b/	buy
/f/	file	/v/	value
/t/	tax	/d/	deal
/θ/	think	/ð/	this
/tʃ/	cheap	/dʒ/	job
/s/	sell	/z/	zero
/k/	card	/g/	gain
/ʃ/	option	/ʒ/	decision

2 Other consonants
/m/	mine	/l/	loss
/n/	net	/r/	rise
/ŋ/	branding	/w/	win
/h/	high	/j/	year

1 Brands

2
/ɪ/ as in quick fix: business; image; management; women
/iː/ as in clean sheet: appeal; believe; increasingly; people

3
sell; sells
launch; launches
cost; costs
use; uses
believe; believes
produce; produces
develop; develops
establish; establishes

4
1 create; creates
2 focus; focuses
3 design; designs
4 raise; raises
5 advertise; advertises
6 face; faces
7 suggest; suggests
8 increase; increases
9 generate; generates
10 endorse; endorses

5
1 Think about our clients. *They're* looking for something that'll make their brand more exciting.
2 *We're* doing a lot of advertising to establish our brand.
3 I just *don't* think we should increase our prices.
4 Well, *I'm* not sure *it's* a good idea to stop manufacturing in Europe.
5 Why *don't* we change our pricing policy?
6 Let's get in touch with Sandra and see if *she's* interested.

6
1 *How about* reducing the price by 15%?
2 *Why don't we* aim our products at young people only?
3 *I think we* should license the whole product range.
4 *How do you feel* about redesigning the packaging?
5 *In my view*, we should devise a new advertising campaign.
6 *I suggest that* we try and project a new image to appeal to a different market segment.

7
1 A: How about reducing the price by 15%?
   B: I'm afraid I can't agree. Our products are already among the cheapest on the market.
2 A: Why don't we aim our products at young people only?
   B: That's a great idea! I think we are focusing on too many segments of the market.
3 A: I think we should license the whole product range.
   B: Maybe, but bear in mind that the 'Made in Finland' label attracts a lot of customers.
4 A: How do you feel about redesigning the packaging?
   B: Mm, good idea. I think it looks rather boring, to be honest.
5 A: In my view, we should devise a new advertising campaign.
   B: I see what you mean, but surely you know how much we already spend on TV commercials.
6 A: I suggest that we try and project a new image to appeal to a different market segment.
   B: Yes, I'd go along with that. But what to change? The logo? The taste?

8
Speaker 1: Dario is taking care of the invitations, so I'm pleased to say that everything is going according to plan. Here are the main details again: the seminar on branding is on Tuesday the 15th, from ten till two, and the venue is the Korona Hotel on Park Avenue. Sandra Delville is a brilliant speaker, so this event should draw a bit of a crowd.

Speaker 2: I suppose our main problem is our packaging. It looks old-fashioned, and I'm sure it has very little appeal for the younger generation. What we should do is some thorough market research, so that we can find out exactly what image we need to project.

Speaker 3: I've heard about your six-month course in marketing, and it sounds very interesting indeed. Considering that I already have some experience in the field, though, I'd need a detailed description of the course syllabus before I decide to go ahead and enrol. Also, anything you can tell me about the degree you award would be very useful.

Speaker 4: This cannot go on. We keep getting calls and letters of complaint from customers concerning our new soft drink. Some even suggest that it has given them stomachache. What I want you to do is first to have this product re-tested immediately, and second, to let me have a detailed report by Friday. Then I'll decide whether to discontinue the line or not.

Speaker 5: We know that Asian consumers believe that top-quality clothes are made in Europe. On the other hand, we are also painfully aware of production costs in Europe. So, we'd like to know what your views are, and what you think the best course of action is. All of us here know that you have a tremendous amount of experience in the field of licensing, so we're eager to listen to you.

2 Travel

9
1 Is Alice <u>wrong</u>?
2 Let's hope it doesn't <u>rain</u>.
3 Were you <u>stressed</u>?
4 Jim was <u>asleep</u> again.
5 It's a Spanish <u>port</u>.
6 Do you know its <u>price</u>?
7 Do you know it's <u>rice</u>?
8 It's a Spanish <u>sport</u>.
9 Jim wants to <u>sleep</u> again.
10 They'd like to <u>rest</u>.
11 The <u>train</u> didn't stop.
12 Is Dennis <u>strong</u>?

10
1 I'll take the high-<u>speed</u> <u>train</u>.
2 There's a <u>problem</u> with our <u>strategy</u>.
3 We're going to <u>train</u> more <u>staff</u>.
4 We'll <u>probably</u> <u>stretch</u> our <u>brand</u>.
5 <u>Steve</u> is <u>flying</u> to <u>Frankfurt</u> on <u>Friday</u>.
6 Our <u>French</u> <u>stores</u> are <u>stylish</u> and <u>spacious</u>.

11
1 They travel by train.
2 It'll cost us a lot more.
3 I'm afraid he'll let us down.
4 We'll visit them every Thursday.
5 You'll go to Frankfurt every week.
6 I leave at six.

12
1 What time do I have to check in? ↘
2 Who will pick her up at the airport? ↘

13
1 When will she be back?
2 How much is a return ticket?
3 Why was your train delayed?
4 How long is the journey?
5 What time is the connecting flight?

14
1 Surely there's an earlier flight, isn't there? ↗
2 This queue doesn't seem to be moving, does it? ↘

15
1 She's going to take an earlier flight back, isn't she? ↘
2 You're not travelling on the night train, are you? ↗
3 We'll get a discount, won't we? ↗
4 You've phoned the travel agency, haven't you? ↘
5 You'll phone in if there's a delay, won't you? ↘
6 Our flight isn't delayed, is it? ↗

16
Message 1: Good afternoon. This is a message from Ralph Knight at Bernardini Fashion. I was calling to let you know that I'll be in Dortmund next week, and I wanted to make an appointment to see you. I'd like to tell you about our new collection. Erm … Well, anyway. I'll call back later or send you an e-mail when I get back to the office.

Message 2: Hello, Julie. Peter here. I finally managed to have a look at the draft programme you produced for our Chinese visitors. You've done a great job as usual. It's looking very good on the whole, except that the schedule for the Friday afternoon seems a bit tight. I'll get a revised version off to you at once. And … talk to you tomorrow.

Message 3: Sandra. Hi. Rachel here. Something urgent's just come up and I have to dash off to Head Office. So I can't make it this afternoon, I'm afraid. I'm very sorry. I'll give you a ring when I get back. Speak to you soon. Bye!

Message 4: This is a message for Mr Benson, Head of Accounts, from Liz Glover in Sales. Today is 3 April, and I see from my bank statement that my February travel expenses haven't been paid in yet. It can't go on like this! Why do we have to talk to a machine and wait ages to have our expenses refunded?

Message 5: This is Rose Wilkinson here, from the Travel Section. I got your note about the hotel booking. I see you're leaving on Tuesday, and it's a two-day conference, but could you specify whether you plan to come back on the Wednesday or the Thursday? Please get back to me and let me know so I can go ahead with the reservation.

3 Change

17
adapted; converted; customised; second; computer; considerably; February

18
1 We've <u>c</u>onverted the stat<u>io</u>n into <u>a</u> hotel.
2 They've <u>a</u>dapted the equip<u>me</u>nt.
3 They've cust<u>o</u>mised the <u>c</u>omputer programs.
4 They've had sec<u>o</u>nd thoughts <u>a</u>bout the project.
5 Things h<u>a</u>ve improved c<u>o</u>nsiderably since Janua<u>ry</u>.

AUDIO SCRIPTS

19
1 She's restructured the company.
2 They've just relocated.
3 He hasn't retrained.
4 We haven't relaunched it yet.
5 Where's he gone?
6 What've they done?

20
1 It's changed enormously.
2 She's redesigned the office.
3 They've moved in the right direction.
4 He hasn't been retrained to use the new equipment.
5 They haven't decentralised the decision-making process.

21
1 Any comments on this? Anything you don't agree with, or anything you'd like to add?
2 As you know, the purpose of this meeting is to inform you about forthcoming changes in our Human Resources department.
3 Great to see so many people here this afternoon. Right. Let's get down to business.
4 We don't want to run over schedule, so let's skip the details and move on to the last key issue.
5 I think we've covered everything, so let's go over the main points briefly.
6 I don't think that's relevant to our discussion.
7 Just let me finish, please, if you don't mind.
8 OK then. Let me stop here and explain that in a bit more detail.
9 OK, let's go over what we've agreed.
10 It's almost nine o'clock and I think everybody's here. Shall we make a start, then?
11 So, how do you feel about this proposal? ... Julia? OK, tell us what you think.
12 Sorry. Just hang on a moment, please. Sylvia hasn't quite finished.
13 Well, that's certainly an interesting issue, but I'm afraid it isn't on today's agenda.
14 We've called this meeting to discuss ways in which we could improve our recruitment strategy.

22
1 A: They complained that the work schedule was too tight.
   B: I'm afraid I didn't quite catch that. What did you say they complained about?
2 A: The interviews will be carried out at our headquarters.
   B: Sorry, where will the interviews be carried out, did you say?
3 A: The job sounded so interesting that 340 people applied for it.
   B: Sorry, I didn't get that. How many people did you say applied for the job?

23
1 Sorry, I didn't get that. Who did you say seems to be the most suitable candidate?
2 Sorry, how long has he worked in Bulgaria for, did you say?
3 I'm afraid I didn't quite catch that. Where did he graduate from?

4 Sorry, I didn't get that. Who did you say he was training?
5 I'm afraid I didn't quite catch that. When does the project finish?

4 Organisation

24
budget; business; consumer; figures; full; purpose

25
1 budget; consultant; customer
2 business; minute; busy
3 consumer; distribute; introduce
4 figures; subsidiary; status
5 full; push; pull
6 purpose; survey; return

26
1 We've got sales offices in over ten countries.
2 He's on a work placement in Italy.

27
1 We want to set up an overseas office in India.
2 Our company's organised in eight divisions.
3 In your opinion, what are the good qualities of our organisation?

28
company; government; interesting; policy
consumer; decision; equipment; department
Japanese; understand

29
1 I work in the travel section.
2 I'm a project manager.
3 My job involves quite a lot of paperwork.
4 I'm responsible for finding new business contacts in the Pacific Rim.
5 I'm in charge of staff training.
6 I spend a lot of time dealing with enquiries.

30
1 I haven't seen you for ages. How's everything going?
2 Frances, I'd like you to meet Greg. He's our new computer expert.
3 Could you let me have their contact details?
4 I hear your trip was very successful.
5 How about you? Still in Human Resources?
6 So your main activity is civil engineering.

5 Advertising

31
no; now   load; loud   a boat; about

32
1 slogan; mouth; poster; phone
2 local; sponsor; growth; notice
3 allow; outline; own; power
4 logo; radio; know; commercial
5 audience; account; town; background

33
1 a clever ad
2 further information
3 a clear idea
4 prepare everything

34

1   She was 'Advertiser of the Year' in 2004.
2   Their adverts were always thought-provoking.
3   Can I have your attention for a moment?
4   The picture is more interesting than the caption.
5   Our agency has hired a star athlete.

35

We advertise on radio, on television, in the papers and

through mailshots.

36

1   We want ads that are clever, eye-catching,

    powerful and inspiring.

2   Our aim is to influence, to seduce and to persuade.

3   I'll give you some background, outline the concept

    and finish with the storyboard.

37

Formal presentation: Good morning, ladies and gentlemen. On behalf of Elgora International, I'd like to welcome you all. Let me introduce myself. My name's Sarah Evans, and I've been managing Elgora's department of international economic relations for the past six years. Thank you for giving me the opportunity to talk to you today. The theme of my presentation is a comparison of the changes in consumer prices in the European Union and the United States from 1999 till today.
I've divided my presentation into three parts. First of all, we'll analyse the pattern of price inflation in the various countries under scrutiny. Secondly, we'll study the main factors responsible for the rise and fall of inflation in the two regions. Finally, we'll look at the forecast for the next two years.

Informal presentation: Hello everyone. I'm Rick Vandermeer. Thanks for this opportunity to talk to you about our new products.
My talk's in three parts. I'll kick off with the findings of the market research that led to the development of our new educational computer games. Then we'll move on to a demo, so that you'll all have a chance to have a go. And we'll finish with your feedback and your ideas and suggestions for our forthcoming advertising campaign.

6 Money

38

1   Let me just go through the figures *for* you.
2   Sales stood *at* two hundred thousand.
3   Profit went up *from* 18 *to* 21 million.
4   Production went down *at* the end *of* the year.
5   Profits rose 6% *to* €9.3 million.
6   This year, orders *from* Russia have levelled off.

39

the fourteenth of July; July fourteenth
the first of May nineteen ninety-nine; May first, nineteen ninety-nine
the twenty-second of April two thousand and nine; April twenty-second, two thousand nine

40

1   the seventeenth of February
2   February seventeenth
3   the twentieth of August two thousand and five
4   June thirtieth, two thousand ten
5   the twenty-third of March nineteen ninety
6   January thirteenth two thousand three
7   the thirtieth of October nineteen ninety-nine
8   the third of September

41

A: So revenues for the quarter increased 12.9 per cent.
B: Sorry, no. I said 12.5 per cent.

42

1   A: Their shares have jumped to three hundred and eighty thousand yen.
    B: Well, my table here says three hundred and eighteen thousand, actually.
2   A: Last month, sales fell to nine hundred and fifty thousand.
    B: Worse than that, I'm afraid. They dropped to eight hundred and fifty thousand.
3   A: Let me just read that back to you, 232 623.
    B: 643 – 232 643.
4   A: We'll meet again on the thirtieth.
    B: Really? I thought we'd agreed on the thirteenth.
5   A: Production has increased by 2,450 units.
    B: Sorry. The exact figure is 2,650.
6   A: Did you say that Accounts is on the eighth floor?
    B: No. It's on the twelfth floor, actually.

43

1   After a sharp fall in January, sales levelled off till the end of the first quarter.
2   Sales decreased slightly in the first month and then gradually recovered.
3   Sales fluctuated in the first two months and then began to show a slight improvement.
4   Sales peaked in January and then fell steadily till the end of March.
5   Sales showed low growth in January but then rose significantly in the next two months.
6   Sales went down steadily throughout the first quarter.

7 Cultures

44

would; know; answer; mustn't; lamb; psychology; should; shouldn't; sign; foreign; listen; island

45

1   They *wouldn't* know what to say.
2   You *mustn't* show the palm of your hand.
3   You *should* write them a thank-you note.
4   You *mustn't* be late for meetings.
5   You *shouldn't* write anything on a business card.

46

1   In the States, you don't have to make a lot of small talk.
2   In Brazil, you have to shake hands with everyone.
3   I'll probably have to invite them over.
4   Don't worry, you won't have to answer questions about your personal life.

47

1 A: Have you told anyone yet?
B: I've told <u>Sandra</u>.
2 A: You should tell Sandra as soon as possible.
B: I <u>have</u> told Sandra.

48

1 A: Do you speak any foreign languages?
B: Well, I can speak <u>Japanese</u>.
2 A: What a pity you can't speak Japanese!
B: But I <u>can</u> speak Japanese.
3 A: You could buy them some chocolates.
B: I've bought them some <u>flowers</u>.
4 A: What about buying them some flowers?
B: I <u>have</u> bought them some flowers.

49

1 A: *Excuse me*. Do you happen to know where Agribank is?
B: Sure. Just a bit further down the road, past the supermarket.
2 A: Have some more lamb.
B: *Not for me thanks*. I usually eat very little meat.
3 A: Would you like to have dinner together tomorrow?
B: *I'm sorry*. I'm afraid we're expecting some relatives tomorrow.
4 A: Come on, stay with us a little longer.
B: Sorry, *I really must get going*. It was very nice talking to you.
5 A: I've just received my MBA.
B: *Congratulations*! That's something we've got to celebrate.
6 A: Sorry, I forgot to bring back that report you lent me.
B: *Never mind*. I don't need it till next Monday.
7 A: Unfortunately, I'll probably be made redundant this winter.
B: *I'm sorry to hear that*. It must be a difficult situation to be in.
8 A: Let me just call the waiter.
B: No, I'll get this. *It's on me*.

50

1 A: Is this your first visit to Egypt?
B: No.
2 A: Is your hotel comfortable?
B: Yes.
3 A: Can I get you a drink?
B: Yes.
4 A: Are you still based in Barcelona?
B: No.

51

Speaker 1: Are you still based in Barcelona?

Speaker 2: Can I get you a drink?

Speaker 3: Did you enjoy the presentation?

Speaker 4: How about lunch together tomorrow?

Speaker 5: I heard you had a good time in Dublin.

Speaker 6: Is this your first visit to Egypt?

Speaker 7: Is your hotel comfortable?

Speaker 8: You know Liz, don't you?

8 Human resources

52

appearance; c**a**reer
contr**a**ct; personal**i**ty
impr**o**ve; fl**u**ent
money; c**o**mpany
pr**o**fits; qu**a**lifications
v**a**cancy; cre**a**tive

53

1 Tell‿us‿about your‿experience‿and qualities.
2 You'll have to liaise with‿our team‿of‿experts.

54

1 I'm fluent‿in‿English‿and‿Arabic.
2 I think‿I'm‿an‿effective planner.
3 I've worked‿as‿an‿adviser‿in‿an‿estate‿agency.
4 I graduated‿in‿economics from the University of‿Alagoas‿in 2006.
5 My current‿employer says‿I've got‿excellent‿interpersonal skills.
6 The salary was‿above‿average but‿I expected‿a more challenging job.

55

pro**mo**tion; dis**cu**ssion; de**ci**sion; situ**a**tion; ex**pre**ssion; super**vi**sion

56

1 qualifi**ca**tions
2 impre**ssi**on
3 con**clu**sion
4 communi**ca**tion
5 moti**va**tion
6 di**vi**sion

57

1 Good afternoon. My name's Emilio Conti.
2 I'd like to speak to Mr Yosuke.
3 Can I leave a message?
4 I'm calling about your advertisement in the *Westland Echo*.
5 Just one moment, please. I'll put you through.
6 Hold on.
7 Could you ask him to call me back tomorrow?
8 I'm afraid Mr Andrade is in a meeting just now.
9 I was wondering if you could give me a little more information.
10 Good morning. How can I help you?

58

/eɪ/ as in pl**ay** s**a**fe: a; h; j; k
/iː/ as in cl**ea**n sh**ee**t: b; c; d; e; g; p; t; v
/e/ as in s**e**ll w**e**ll: f; l; m; n; s; x; z
/aɪ/ as in m**y** pr**i**ce: i; y
/əʊ/ as in g**o** sl**ow**: o
/uː/ as in sch**oo**l r**u**les: q; u; w
/ɑː/ as in sm**ar**t c**ar**d: r

59

Excerpt 1

A: Great. And which company are you calling from?
B: I work for Axcentis Financial Consultants in Frankfurt.
A: Erm. Sorry, I didn't catch that.
B: Axcentis. Let me just spell it for you. That's A-X-C-E-N-T-I-S. The full name is Axcentis Financial Consultants, and our offices are in Frankfurt.

Excerpt 2

A: Hello. My name's Manuel Saraiva. That's S-A-R-A-I-V-A.
B: Hi. And how can I help you, Mr Saraiva?

Excerpt 3

A: So I'll go over the name of the street again: Zeleny Pruh. That's Z-E-L-E-N-Y, new word, P-R-U-H, number 25b.

B: And that's in Prague, isn't it?

A: That's right. Prague 4.

Excerpt 4

A: Thank you so much for these details, Ms Hirano. I'd just like to check how you spell your first name. Is that S-A-Y-

B: Sorry, no. Seiya is spelt S-E-I-Y-A. Would you like me to go over it once more?

Excerpt 5

A: I've got the name of the company all right, but I'd like to check how you spell Barroquinha. Is that B-A-double R-O-Q-U-I-N-H-A?

B: Yes. That's correct.

Excerpt 6

A: Their Tokyo office address is 131, Roppongi, Minato-ku, Tokyo.

B: Sorry. How do you spell Roppongi?

A: That's R-O-double P-O-N-G-I.

B: I've got that. Thanks.

Excerpt 7

A: So, my name is Roberto Ruiz.

B: Sorry. Did you say Reyes?

A: No, Ruiz. R-U-I-Z.

Excerpt 8

A: I've looked everywhere for Mr Irkut's file and I can't find it!

B: Let me see. Ah! But why are you looking under 'i'? You've got the spelling wrong.

A: Really?

B: Yeah! You should be looking under 'u'. The name's Urquhart. That's U-R-Q-U-H-A-R-T.

A: Oh dear! Who would've thought?

60

1 A: So your office is at 36, Wellington Street.
   B: No. It's Wellington <u>Road</u>, in fact.

2 A: The interview is on the twenty-first, is that right?
   B: Sorry, no. It's on the twenty-<u>third</u>.

3 A: ... and your agent in St Petersburg is Konstantin Bupnov. B-U-P-N- ...
   B: Sorry, that's spelt B-U-<u>B</u>-N-O-V.

4 A: And you graduated from the University of Almeria four years ago.
   B: Well, that was <u>five</u> years ago, actually.

9 International markets

61

1	goods	5	prompt
2	first	6	sixth
3	contract	7	against
4	lunch	8	next

62

1	belts and wallets	5	tax-exempt
2	needs and wants	6	self-employment
3	imports and exports	7	a sales forecast
4	interest rates	8	a bulk discount

63

1 A: Long-term prospe<u>cts</u> aren'<u>t</u> bright, are they?
   B: No. In fa<u>ct</u>, mo<u>st</u> economi<u>sts</u> foreca<u>st</u> a slum<u>p</u>.

2 A: Their new ra<u>nge</u> of produ<u>cts</u> is quite impressive.
   B: Yeah. I particularly like their sp<u>orts</u> jacke<u>ts</u> and their si<u>lk</u> scar<u>ves</u>.

3 A: Is it true the sa<u>les</u> confere<u>nce</u> has been cancelle<u>d</u>?
   B: No. I<u>t's</u> ju<u>st</u> been postpo<u>ned</u> till the fi<u>fth</u> of Augu<u>st</u>.

4 A: So they offer a 2.5-per-cent discou<u>nt</u> for pro<u>mpt</u> payme<u>nt</u>?
   B: Tha<u>t's</u> right, yes. But I do<u>n't</u> know if their price incl<u>udes</u> insura<u>nce</u>.

5 A: We have<u>n't</u> met our sa<u>les</u> targe<u>ts</u> yet.
   B: Maybe not, but we've establi<u>shed</u> excelle<u>nt</u> relationshi<u>ps</u> with our age<u>nts</u>.

6 A: To be hone<u>st</u>, I thought our fir<u>st</u> conta<u>ct</u> was rather diffic<u>ult</u>.
   B: Well, why do<u>n't</u> you arra<u>nge</u> to have lu<u>nch</u> with them ne<u>xt</u> time?

64

I'll try.	He**'ll** accept.
She **won't** sign.	They **won't** accept.
We**'d** refuse.	They**'d** agree.
It **wouldn't** happen.	She **wouldn't** answer.

65

1 We'll look for another supplier.
2 She'd agree to sign.
3 I won't accept their offer.
4 They'd try someone else.
5 He'll get a high discount.
6 You'd have no choice.
7 It wouldn't arrive on time.
8 You'll have to agree.
9 It'll be difficult.
10 We won't sign.

66

1 If you give us a more substantial discount, we'll place a larger order.
2 Provided that you can cover insurance, we'll sign the deal.
3 Unless you agree to split transport costs, we won't be able to place a firm order.
4 As long as you can deliver this month, there won't be any problems.
5 Providing the price is right, we'll buy everything you produce.

67

Speaker 1: I'm afraid that if you can't cover insurance, we can't accept your offer.

Speaker 2: It all seems fine to me, but I'd like to get back to you about this a bit later. I need to consult my colleagues.

Speaker 3: Of course, if you were willing to increase your order, we'd be prepared to offer you a better price.

Speaker 4: When you said we'd get a 10% discount, did you mean on an order of 100, or more?

Speaker 5: Would you be prepared to guarantee an earlier delivery date? How would you feel about that?

10 Ethics

68

1	result; corruption	4	industrial; customer
2	drug; company	5	discuss; money
3	country; month	6	government; unfair

69

1 A: Helen was always taking extended lunch breaks, wasn't she?
  B: Yeah, and she was phoning in sick almost every week.

2 A: What they were doing wasn't really unethical.
  B: Well, if you ask me, I'd say that it was.

3 A: The previous owners weren't exactly trustworthy.
  B: Weren't they?

4 A: Was he as corrupt as his predecessor?
  B: Yes, he was. Even more so.

5 A: Were those investments considered ethical?
  B: Of course they were.

6 A: There was a bit of a cover-up, wasn't there?
  B: There certainly was. And a major one at that.

70

1 They'd already launched the new model, hadn't they?
2 They were losing money, weren't they?
3 It wasn't really going well, was it?
4 She hadn't done anything wrong, had she?
5 He'd been discriminated against, *hadn't* he?
6 It *was* a big scandal, wasn't it?
7 We weren't putting pressure on him to resign, *were* we?
8 They *hadn't* bribed anyone, had they?

71

Speaker 1: All right everyone? What we're going to do then is to forbid smoking on all our premises.

Speaker 2: Doing nothing would have disastrous consequences for our reputation.

Speaker 3: In the circumstances, I think it is advisable to follow a new course of action.

Speaker 4: My solution, then, is to stop hiring anyone on recommendations from our own staff.

Speaker 5: When you say that staff shouldn't be allowed to spend time making personal phone calls during working hours, I agree with you in principle, but then we know that some people have very good reasons to do so.

Speaker 6: Well, you could be right, but it's not a particularly safe strategy.

Speaker 7: Restricting access to the Internet is very likely to make a lot of our staff unhappy.

Speaker 8: What we need to do is look at the situation from the perspective of our customers themselves. We really should be looking at this from a different angle.

72

1 I'm not sure I trust our new accountant. To me, all those errors seem deliberate. Any *idea* how we should address this issue?

2 She's very worried about frauds with government contracts. *Don't* you think we should do something about it?

3 He keeps telling me that his cousin would be the best person for the job. What *shall* we do?

4 Tim's already taken five days of sick leave this month. What do you think we *should* do?

5 The new office manager is putting pressure on Elaine to go out with him. What do you *suggest* we do?

73

1 A: I'm not sure I trust our new accountant. To me, all those errors seem deliberate. Any idea how we should address this issue?
  B: If I were you, I'd give her another chance. Honestly, she doesn't look the type of person who'd make false entries in the accounts.

2 A: She's very worried about frauds with government contracts. Don't you think we should do something about it?
  B: I think we should tell her not to speak to anyone. The issue's far too serious.

3 A: He keeps telling me that his cousin would be the best person for the job. What shall we do?
  B: Let's just tell him it's not on. There's no room for corruption in our company.

4 A: Tim's already taken five days of sick leave this month. What do you think we should do?
  B: Have you thought of confronting him with the issue? He may have genuine health problems.

5 A: The new office manager is putting pressure on Elaine to go out with him. What do you suggest we do?
  B: I suggest you check his personnel record first. Find out if he's ever been accused of harassment.

11 Leadership

74

1 term; person; working
2 refer; assertive; expertise
3 turn; entrepreneur; interpret
4 reserved; world; firm

75

1 Jim's‿awfully worried‿about‿it.
2 I don't‿agree with‿Alan‿at‿all.

76

1 It's the main‿item‿on‿our‿agenda.
2 First‿of‿all, could you give‿us the background?
3 We need more‿information‿about this‿issue.
4 Here‿are some‿ideas for‿us to think‿about.
5 They haven't thought‿about‿all the details.

77

1 She was de<u>ci</u>sive, cre<u>a</u>tive and highly ar<u>ti</u>culate.
2 He was en<u>cou</u>raging, dy<u>na</u>mic and extremely ide<u>a</u>listic.
3 She was <u>prin</u>cipled, rea<u>lis</u>tic and very <u>cas</u>ual.
4 He was <u>dis</u>tant, con<u>ser</u>vative and unspeakably <u>ruth</u>less.
5 She was <u>cau</u>tious, <u>hum</u>ble and rather re<u>served</u>.

78

1 Before I *move* on to the next part of my talk, are there any questions on what I've said so far?

2 Good morning everyone. *I'm* delighted *to be here today*. My name's Dharamjit Singh.

3 I'm sure *you're all aware* that some modifications must be made to the design.

4 If it's all right, I'll *deal with* questions at the end of my presentation.
5 If there are no more questions, thank you again for *your attention*.
6 Thank you all for coming. Before we start, *I'd just like to say* a few words about myself.
7 Thanks for being such *a great audience*. I hope we meet again at our next convention.

79

[I = Interviewer; **MC** = Management Consultant]

I Making decisions is something most of us do every day. It is also something most of us very often dislike doing. This begs the question 'Why is that so?'

MC Part of the answer lies in the fact that any decision we make involves a certain amount of risk; it can have good or bad consequences. It is in our human nature to want to do the best we can, and we are afraid of failure. In fact, many people often refuse to make a decision, or postpone it indefinitely, simply for fear of the consequences.
Paralysed by fear, they are led to the wrong conclusion that doing nothing is necessarily better than making a bad decision. Therefore, it is of crucial importance to accept the fact that there is no such thing as a perfect decision.
Deciding involves choosing; choosing between different courses of action. In many ways, when we are faced with a choice, we should be grateful.

I What exactly do you mean?

MC I mean that whenever I make a decision, I become a more responsible agent, I shape events instead of allowing myself to be shaped by them.

I Of course we can't predict the consequences of our actions with full accuracy. Does that mean though that decision-making is like gambling?

MC Fortunately, it isn't. There are a number of principles which seem to guide effective decision-makers.

I For example?

MC The first step is to make sure we really understand the situation to which we are trying to respond through our decision. This involves gathering information and listening to other people involved.
Secondly, we need to brainstorm all the possible choices we have at our disposal. At this stage, we need to be daring, creative and adventurous, so we are able to come up with choices that weren't at all obvious at the beginning.

I I see what you mean. But presumably you also need to evaluate these choices?

MC Absolutely. And this is precisely the third step in the process. It is clear that some of the solutions listed in step two will be more realistic and more adequate than others.

I What sort of questions do I ask myself at this evaluation stage?

MC Well, for example, What difference will my choice make? Who will it affect, and How will it affect them? If necessary, can I go back on my decision? etc. etc.

I These guiding principles do sound extremely interesting but also very time-consuming. If I go through all three preliminary stages before I act, do I not run the risk of missing the boat, as it were?

MC Time is of course a key issue. But in fact, it may take a good leader less time to go through those guiding principles than it took me to describe them! Those principles are meant precisely to speed up the process.
Finally, let's not forget that very often, the best decision is the timeliest one.

I So it's clearly a question of doing the right thing at the right time.

12 Competition

80

short course; go slow; lawn; loan

81

1	call	5	focus
2	cause	6	horse
3	cope	7	goal
4	drawn	8	store

82

1 *They'd* try to dominate the market.
2 We *want to* overtake Samsung.
3 *I'll* listen to the news.
4 I'm sure *they* like the exhibition.
5 We know you *won't* take the company upmarket.
6 I don't think *you* agree.

83

compete; competitor; competition; competitive
innovate; innovator; innovation; innovative
invent; inventor; invention; inventive
create; creator; creation; creative
protect; protector; protection; protective

84

1 A: So we'll hold our next meeting in June.
   B: Wouldn't September be better?
2 A: Of course, we'll order from Wilson's as usual.
   B: Shouldn't we try another supplier this time?
3 A: They just agreed to a 10% discount for orders of 100 items or more.
   B: Couldn't we insist on better terms?
4 A: Let's ask Crawley Engineering for a quote.
   B: Aren't they too expensive?
5 A: I think we should cancel the deal at once.
   B: Hadn't we better wait a few more days?
6 A: We can deliver in 45 days, not 30 as they expect.
   B: Won't they be disappointed?
7 A: I'll ask Mark if he wants to negotiate this contract.
   B: Wouldn't it be better to ask Jenny?

85

1 *Could you possibly give* us 30 days' credit?
2 *I'm afraid I can't* deliver in ten days.
3 We were *expecting* a bigger order.
4 *Unfortunately*, we aren't *in a position* to give you any credit.
5 We *might not be able* to do that.
6 *I'm sorry* to inform you that you haven't won the contract.